MONEY IN SIXTEENTH-CENTURY FLORENCE

CARLO M. CIPOLLA

Money in Sixteenth-Century Florence

University of California Press
Berkeley • Los Angeles • London

Originally published in Italian as
La moneta a Firenze nel Cinquecento

University of California Press
Berkeley and Los Angeles, California
University of California Press, Ltd.
London, England

Library of Congress Cataloging-in-Publication Data

Cipolla, Carlo M.
Money in sixteenth-century Florence / Carlo M. Cipolla.
p. cm.
Bibliography: p.
Includes index.
ISBN 0-520-06222-1 (alk. paper)
1. Money—Italy—Florence—History—16th century. I. Title.
HG1040.F55C565 1989 89-30545
332.4'94551—dc19 CIP

1 2 3 4 5 6 7 8 9

Contents

Illustrations

Tables

Preface

The second half of the sixteenth century saw interesting events in the money and financial markets of Florence. The consequences of the arrival of massive quantities of silver from the Americas and the problems it caused were exacerbated in Florence by the grand duke's insistence on having the last word in monetary policy. A complex situation was further complicated during the 1570s and 1580s by the unfolding of a banking crisis that had its origins not only in technical matters but also in political interference and personality conflicts. In other words, this book, which sets out to deal with purely technical matters, ends by straying into the political, social, and administrative history of sixteenth-century Florence.

Paradoxically, more is known of Florentine and Tuscan monetary history for the Middle Ages than for the early modern period. Even today anyone wishing to study Florentine coinage in the sixteenth century, apart from the present study, has to rely either on the seventeenth-century study by Orsini or Arrigo Galeotti's work published in 1930. Both are numismatic in their approach and, however praiseworthy for the times in which they were published, nevertheless suffer from errors and lack of precision.[1]

1. Orsini, *Storia delle monete*; and Galeotti, *Monete del Granducato di Toscana*. References in this and the following footnotes are abbreviated. Full references are given in the Bibliography.

The subject has been dealt with fleetingly in recent years by three different authors, who, because of their own different research interests, have neglected the great mass of accounts existing in the mint archives.[2]

In the sixteenth century—the century of fabulous treasures from Peru and Mexico—minting in Italy can be studied for protracted periods in the Florentine market alone. In Genoa most of the documents have been destroyed; from the few fragments that have survived it is possible to evaluate the production of the Genoan mint for only a few years here and there: data that in fact tell us little or nothing.[3] In Milan the minting registers have been destroyed; continuous series of coinages of the Milanese mint are available only from 1580, thanks to the transcription, albeit less than perfect, of an eighteenth-century antiquarian.[4] For Venice, an expert on the subject has concluded that "no usable data exist for the first seventy or eighty years of the sixteenth century."[5] The archive of the Florentine mint is far from a model of order and precision, but with infinite patience the various pieces of the mosaic can be put together and

2. The monetary system of sixteenth-century Florence was taken up in 1939 by Giuseppe Parenti in his book *Prime ricerche sulla rivoluzione dei prezzi in Firenze*. In a few lucid pages he established the silver parity of the unit of account in order to change the accounting expression of prices into grams of silver. Tondo's "Moneta nella storia d'Europa del '500" is worthless for economic questions.

In 1984 Paolozzi-Strozzi traced a brief profile of the Medici coins in the booklet *Monete fiorentine dalla Repubblica ai Medici*. This is a lucid guide to the collections of coins in the Bargello Museum.

3. Meroni, *Libri delle uscite delle monete*, p. ix. See also Pesce and Felloni, *Monete genovesi*, p. 2.

4. Argelati, *De monetis Italiae*, vol. 3, app. See also Cipolla, *Mouvements monétaires*.

5. Tucci, "Emissioni monetarie di Venezia," in *Mercanti, navi, monete nel Cinquecento veneziano*, p. 300.

a reasonably continuous series of issues of coins assembled. Nonetheless, the last chapter clearly shows that mint data alone, even as substantial as in Florence, can be misleading if not supplemented from other sources. In the case of Florence, these supplementary sources are also available.

It has not been simple to study and describe the monetary and banking developments of sixteenth-century Florence. Complex problems have had to be clarified, and an enormous number of intricate documents have had to be interpreted. This is decidedly not an easy book. I have done my best, however, to render a subject generally considered abstruse accessible to the non-specialist, and I hope to have presented, as lucidly as possible, results that are something of a historiographical novelty.

I wish to thank Professor E. Stumpo and Dr. G. Pallanti for information about archival material, and the staff of the Archivio di Stato di Firenze, in particular Paola Peruzzi and Teresa Arnoldo, for having facilitated my archival research by their courtesy and solicitude. Julia Bamford provided the translation from the original Italian edition. All coins illustrated below, with the sole exception of the Spanish piece of eight, are reproduced by permission of the Museo Nazionale del Bargello, Florence.

Florence, April 1986

CHAPTER ONE

Coins: Their Types and Denominations

WHEN LORENZO the Magnificent died in 1492, the system of metallic currency prevailing in Florence was still of a medieval type, in the sense that practically the same system had already existed for the past one or two hundred years. There were three sorts of coins: (1) a gold coin represented by the gold fiorino (florin); (2) silver coins represented by the grossi (groats); and (3) the biglione, that is, coins of very base silver represented by the quattrino and the denaro (popularly known as picciolo). In addition, the circulation of certain coins from states near and far was more or less tolerated.

To all intents and purposes the gold fiorino kept the same weight (around 3.5 grams) and fineness (24 carats) with which it made its debut in 1252. The silver content of the grosso was gradually reduced; however, the fineness remained unchanged at the theoretical level of 958.333/1000 (the so-called lega del popolino) and the progressive deterioration of the coin only appeared in variations in its weight.[1] This deterioration was usually

1. In the metrological language of the time, "popolino" fineness was defined as 11 1/2 ounces, meaning that out of a pound weight (12 ounces)

masked by the minting of ever heavier grossi whose nominal value was increased more than proportionally, so that the coin contained a lesser quantity of silver per unit of value (see table 1). The biglione currency was, as we have said, composed of quattrini and denari whose metallic value had been gradually diminished by the progressive reduction in weight and fineness.[2]

Where the Florentine metallic money system appeared decidedly démodé was in the silver currency. In the second half of the fifteenth century, important silver deposits were discovered and worked in southern Germany, more specifically in the Tyrol and Saxon Bohemia. The silver produced there not only supplied and enlarged local circulation, but also and in great quantities reached the markets of northern Italy (including Florence), with which southern Germany had intense trade relations. The greater quantity of metal

---

of metal, 11 1/2 ounces had to be of pure silver. The ratio 11 1/2:12 corresponds to 958.333/1000 in the metric system. In practice, the available refining techniques did not permit the accuracy we are used to in industrial society. At the beginning of 1577, for example, it was declared that "the money minted in the past six months [September 1576–February 1577] has been of 11 ounces 11 7/8 denari," that is, 957.899/1000 (Archivio di Stato di Firenze [ASF], Zecca 137, c. 24). In August 1590 it was declared, more explicitly, that "the money that is minted should be of 11 ounces 12 denari per pound fineness, but since the fineness can not be perfectly adjusted, we admit that up to 11 ounces 11 denari [954.861/1000] may be legally spent, and all the silver minted in this period [1585–90] has been estimated at 11 ounces 11 3/4 denari of fineness" (that is, 957.465/1000) (ASF, Sindaci 21, ins. 27, doc. 18, August 1590).

Throughout this book the modern system of dating is used, in which the year begins on 1 January, rather than the Florentine system in which the year began on 25 March.

2. See Bernocchi, *Monete della Repubblica*, vol. 3.

TABLE 1. The progressive devaluation of the Florentine silver grosso and its repercussions on the silver parity of the Florentine lira of account (lira di piccioli).

Year	Approximate number of lire of piccioli extracted in the form of grossi from 1 lb. of popolino silver	Gm and tenths of gm of pure silver (1000/1000) equivalent to 1 lira of piccioli on the basis of silver content and the value of the grosso	Exchange rate of the gold florin expressed in soldi and denari piccioli
1306	17	19.0	52.10
1318	21	15.7	61
1345	26	12.3	62–62.8
1347	29	11.1	60–62.8
1368	30	10.8	65.8
1390	34	9.6	74.9–76.6
1402	36	9.0	75.9–76.8
1425	37	8.8	79.6–80.8
1461	43	7.6	101.10
1471	47	6.9	110
1481	49	6.6	120
1503	60	5.4	140
1506	61	5.4	140
1530	64	5.2	140
1531	68	4.9	150

SOURCE: Bernocchi, *Monete della Repubblica*.

available encouraged the coinage of heavier coins. In 1472 the Venetian mint, followed by the Milanese mint two years later, issued silver coins that broke with the medieval tradition on two fronts. In a formal and artistic departure, the Venetian coin bore the image of the doge Tron, while the Milanese bore that of the duke Galeazzo Maria Sforza.[3] Both portraits were vividly realistic and of a clearly Renaissance stamp. From the point of view of substance, the two coins differed radically from the thin medieval coins on account of their thickness and consequently their weight and silver content. The new Venetian money weighed 6.52 grams with a fineness of 948/1000.[4] The new Milanese money weighed 9.79 grams with a fineness of 963.5/1000.[5] These parameters had nothing in common with the parameters of the various grossi in circulation, whose weight was around 2 grams in the case of the heavier coins.[6]

The example of Venice and Milan was quickly followed by the other mints in northern Italy. Silver pieces of over 9 grams were minted in 1483 in Piedmont and Savoy and from 1490–91 in Genoa.[7] In Ferrara in 1493,

3. The innovation of placing a realistic portrait of the doge on coins clashed with popular democratic feelings in Venice, so much so that when the doge Tron died, it was decided that the effigy of the doge should appear only symbolically, in the form of an indistinguishable person kneeling before St. Mark, as had been done in the past coinages of the gold ducat.

4. Papadopoli, *Monete di Venezia*, vol. 2, pp. 3–4, 8–10, 571 doc. 39.

5. Cipolla, *Moneta a Milano*.

6. In Florence the grosso coined in 1481 and 1489 and valued at 6 soldi 8 denari weighed 2.3 grams; those coined in 1503, valued at 7 soldi, weighed 2 grams; those coined in 1531 and valued at 7 soldi 6 denari weighed 1.9 grams. They were all of 958.33/1000 fineness.

7. For Piedmont and Savoy, see Promis, *Monete dei Reali di Savoia*, vol. 1, pp. 147, 155, 492; for Genoa, see Pesce and Felloni, *Monete genovesie*, p. 258.

the duke Ercole d'Este had a piece minted weighing 7.7 grams, so beautiful that it looked more like a medal than a coin.[8] All the above pieces were referred to as testoni (testoons), for the bust of the ruler appearing on them.

Not until 1503, during the first Republic, did Florence decide to mint a silver coin of approximately the same weight as the testoni. This venture began timidly, with the so-called quinto di scudo, a piece weighing 7.7 grams, that is, similar to Ercole d'Este's testone. On its appearance it was given the value of 1 lira 8 soldi. Limited quantities were minted and, as we shall see, it was short-lived. The year following the appearance of the quinto di scudo, in August 1504, the Florentine mint began producing a silver coin that was between the grosso and the testone in its metallic content. This new coin was initially called carlino or barile because it represented the exact amount needed to pay the duty for a barrel of wine at the city gates.[9] The decree that ordered the minting of this coin specified as the reason for the new coin "that its value should represent precisely that which must be paid for a barrel of wine." If the immediate reason was the creation of a monetary unit suitable for paying the duty on wine, nevertheless the name with which it was first christened (carlino) and its numismatic characteristics hint at a more distant and deeper origin.[10]

The silver carlino that first appeared in the Kingdom of Naples in 1278, at the time of Charles I of Anjou, weighed 3.3 grams with a fineness of 934/1000. Despite the fact that its coinage was often interrupted, the

8. Grierson, *Ercole d'Este*, essay XVII, p. 41.

9. Bernocchi, *Monete della Repubblica*, vol. 1, p. 427.

10. The text of the ordinance that authorized the minting of this coin specifically states "that in the said mint should be issued . . . a new silver coin . . . called grossone or carlino" (ibid.).

Neapolitan carlino was kept at between 3 and 4 grams during the following centuries and remained the basic unit of the Neapolitan monetary system. The popularity of the coin was such, even outside the Kingdom of Naples, that Rome, which had close economic and financial relations with Naples, adopted the carlino as the basic unit of the pontifical monetary system. The papal carlino, also known as papal grosso, and from 1501 as giulio in honor of Pope Julius II, stayed at between 3 and 3.7 grams in weight.

As has been mentioned, in August 1504 Florence decided to mint the silver coin that was at first called carlino, and then, popularly, barile, and finally—following the Roman example—giulio. The fineness was the sacred Florentine one of the "popolino," that is, 958.333/1000. Its weight was fixed at 3.512 grams; consequently, the content was 3.37 grams of fine silver. The nominal value of the new coin was fixed at 10 soldi of "white quattrini," which meant 12 soldi and 6 denari piccioli.[11]

Both the name and the weight and fineness indicate the Neapolitan and Roman origin of this new Florentine piece. The choice of model was in all likelihood dictated by the intensity of economic and financial relations that traditionally linked Florence to Naples and Rome. Whatever the reasons, it is certain that the coin in question

11. Ibid., p. 475; vol. 3, p. 236. Bernocchi (vol. 3, p. 234) draws on Vettori (*Fiorino*, p. 407) for the information that in 1504, 4 quattrini bianchi were the equivalent of 5 quattrini neri. If this was the exchange rate current in 1504, it follows that "10 soldi of white quattrini" were the equivalent of 12 soldi 6 denari of piccioli. A contemporary *Diario* in manuscript form, traced later (ASF, Bardi, sez. 3, b. 14) confirms that on 1 October 1530, in Florence, the carlino-barile was worth 12 soldi 6 denari. In 1531 the exchange rate was brought to 3 quattrini bianchi = 4 quattrini neri (Bernocchi, *Monete della Repubblica*, vol. 1, p. 476; vol. 3, p. 244).

was a success and played the same role in the sixteenth and seventeenth centuries that the grosso had played in the previous centuries.

The carlino-barile-giulio was dragged along with other silver coins into the double devaluation of 1530 and 1531, which will be discussed further in chapter 3: as table 2 shows, the content of fine silver was reduced to 3.30 grams while the nominal value was increased to 13 soldi 4 denari.

In March 1535, the duke Alessandro de' Medici, who had seized power in Florence a few years before, issued a general decree to regulate the entire monetary and payments system. In the case in point, he put a stop to the coining of the glorious and traditional grosso, and the giulio was made the kingpin of the Florentine silver monetary system (fig. 1). The giulio, it was emphatically declared, "must be the money with which usually to negotiate and contract." The metallic content was slightly retouched, bringing it to 3.21 grams of pure silver, while its value of 13 soldi 4 denari was unchanged. Moreover, the coining of a multiple and submultiple, that is to say a piece worth three giulii and a piece worth half a giulio, was decreed.[12] Since the value of the giulio was, as we have seen, 13 soldi and 4 denari (160 denari), the multiple of 3 giulii was equivalent to 480 denari, that is, exactly 2 lire. This piece weighed about 10 grams and was coined at the usual popolino fineness (953.333/1000). On the obverse was the bust of Duke Alessandro with the inscription "Alexander.Med.–R.P.Floren.Dux." It was therefore given the name testone (see fig. 2).[13] It

12. ASF, Zecca, Fiorinaio, cc. 184v ff. See also Cantini, *Legislazione toscana*, vol. 1, p. 84, which gives an incorrect version of the ordinance.

13. The dies of this coin were the work of Benvenuto Cellini, who in chapter 80 of his autobiography wrote with typical immodesty:

TABLE 2. The intrinsic characteristics of the Florentine giulio, 1504–97.

Year	Theoretical fineness (parts per thousand)	Taglio (no. pieces extracted from 1 lb. of popolino silver)	*Resa* (no. pieces mint gave to merchants for 1 lb. of popolino silver)	Theoretical weight (gm and hundredths of a gm of popolino silver)	Pure silver content (gm and hundredths of a gm of pure silver)	Exchange rate (soldi and denari piccioli)	Source
1504	958.33	96.66	94.33	3.51	3.37	12.6	Bernocchi, vol. 3, 236
1531	958.33	98.74		3.44	3.30	13.4	Bernocchi, vol. 3, 244–47
1535	958.33	101.25	99.0	3.35	3.21	13.4	Fiorinaio, 184–85

1538	958.33	105.5	103.15	3.22	3.08	13.4	Fiorinaio, 188v
1543	958.33	106.1		3.20	3.07	13.4	Zecca, 150
1548	958.33	106.3		3.20	3.07	13.4	Zecca, 150
1550	958.33	106.5		3.19	3.05	13.4	Zecca, 150
1552	958.33	107.6		3.16	3.02	13.4	Zecca, 150
1570	958.33	110.3		3.08	2.95	13.4	Zecca, 90
1571	958.33	109.5	106.9	3.10	2.97	13.4	Fiorinaio, 190–91 e Zecca, 90
1597	958.33	109.5	106.9	3.10	2.97	13.4	Fiorinaio, 191–92

NOTE: The difference between taglio and yield represented the cost of coinage (*brassaggio*) plus the seigniorage. The weight has been calculated by dividing the weight of the pound by the taglio. The pure metal content has been calculated by multiplying the weight by the fineness.

FIG. 1. Barile (giulio) of Alessandro de' Medici.

O. ALEXANDER · MED · R · P · FLOREN · DVX ·
R. S · IOANNES · — · BAPTISTA ·
AØ2.6 3.4g

FIG. 2. The testone of Alessandro de' Medici.

O. ALEXANDER · M · — · R · P · FLOREN · DVX ·
R. · S · COSMVS– · S · DAMIANUS ·
AØ2.8 10g

made any further minting of the quinto di scudo useless and thus put an end to the latter's brief life. As Paolozzi Strozzi has written,

> Up to that time and for the whole of the fifteenth century the portrait had been characteristic of medals, which were artistic creations, of great prestige but essentially private. With Cellini's testone of Alessandro, the currency no longer belongs to the City but to the Prince; it has to represent his power, cause his image on it to be admired. It has therefore to be produced by the greatest artist, and no longer by an artisan who is only capable of scrupulously keeping to an inherited prototype. The contrast not only between Cellini and Bastiano Cennini but also between Alessandro, who supported the former, and powerful men such as Ottaviano de' Medici, who in supporting the latter defended tradition, is substantial. It announces the end of the money of Florence, which becomes the money of the Medici.[14]

Once a coin with the nominal value of exactly 2 lire had been minted, it was quite naturally followed a few

---

"I went to visit Duke Lessandro [*sic*] . . . who immediately ordered me to make the dies of his coins, and the first that I made was a coin of 40 soldi with the head of his excellency on the one side and Saint Cosimo and Saint Damiano on the other. These were silver coins, and the Duke was so pleased with them that he ventured to say that they were the most beautiful coins in Christendom."

Galeotti reproduces a piece from a manuscript diary, according to which "the minting of coins of 40 soldi each began, with on the one side the head of Duke Alessandro and on the obverse Saints Cosimo and Damiano, and the dies were made by Benvenuto Cellini" (*Monete del Granducato di Toscana*, p. 24).

14. Paolozzi-Strozzi, *Moneta fiorentina*, p. 56. See also Tondo, *Moneta nella storia d'Europa*, p. 298.

years later, probably in 1539, by a silver coin equivalent to half a testone, that is, with a nominal value of 1 lira. When it first appeared, this coin weighed about 4.8 grams, at a popolino fineness and with a content of about 4.6 grams of pure silver.[15] The coin was baptized a "Cosimo" in honor of the new duke.

The biglione coins consisted of crazie, white quattrini, black quattrini, and denari, known as piccioli. The crazia was a large whitened quattrino the equivalent of 20 denari piccioli. The white quattrino differed from the black quattrino because of the slightly better alloy that gave it a lighter look. In 1531 3 white quattrini were the equivalent of 4 black quattrini.[16] This ratio was still extant in 1545.[17] The black quattrino, which had a nominal value of 4 denari piccioli, was, as its name suggests, a poor ugly coin, weighing less than a gram and made almost entirely of copper:[18] it was a heritage of the Middle Ages, as was also the denaro picciolo, which was coined only occasionally and in small quantities.

Let us turn to gold. The glorious gold coin of Florentine tradition had been the fiorino (florin). Both the weight and the fineness of the fiorino remained practically unaltered during the course of the centuries. The coin had seen its greatest splendor in the period

15. The text of the ordinance of 26 August 1539 is to be found in the Fiorinaio (ASF, Zecca) on c. 188v, but in an incomplete and incorrect form.

16. Bernocchi, *Monete della Repubblica*, vol. 1, p. 476 and vol. 3, p. 244.

17. ASF, Zecca 150.

18. Ninety-three percent of the weight of the black quattrino was copper. Although silver formed only 7 percent of the total weight, it represented around 75 percent of the nominal value of the coin. The copper represented about 5 percent, and coinage expenses and seigniorage the remaining 20 percent. The calculations are based on the mint accounts of 1543–66 (ibid.).

between 1252, the year of its appearance, and the great crisis of the 1340s. During the fifteenth century the fiorino lost its preeminent position, and the ducato (ducat), Venetian in origin but imitated in many other states and similar in intrinsic value to the fiorino, asserted itself as the more popular gold coin on the European scene. At the end of the fifteenth century, even in Florence the florin, though unchanged in weight, fineness, or design, was often referred to as a ducato.

In the first decades of the sixteenth century fashion changed, and the most common type of gold coin in Europe became the écu of French origin. The écu was slightly inferior in weight and fineness to both the fiorino and the ducato: its content of pure gold was around 6 percent less.[19]

Genoa was the first state in Italy to mint gold écus (or scudi), beginning in 1508. The city was under French occupation, and the espousal of the gold scudo by the Genoese monetary authorities was undoubtedly influenced by the political situation. The Genoese scudo of 1508 had a weight of 3.43 grams, a fineness of 22.5

19. The following were the characteristics of the écu au soleil:

	Weight (gm)	Fineness (carats)	Pure gold content (gm)
Reign of Charles VIII:			
August 1494	3.496	23.125	3.37
Reign of Francis I:			
January 1515	3.496	23.125	3.37
May 1519	3.423	22.75	3.25
July 1519	3.439	23.00	3.30

See Blanchet and Dieudonné, *Manuel de numismatique*, vol. 2, pp. 298, 303, 314.

carats, and therefore a content of 3.22 grams of pure gold.[20] The situation was similar in Milan: at an unknown date around 1520, the French king Francois I, having taken power in the city, had a gold scudo coined weighing 3.5 grams with a fineness of 22 carats and a content of 3.21 grams of pure gold.[21] Venice followed suit, beginning to mint a gold scudo in 1528. The new Venetian coin weighed 3.40 grams with a fineness of 22 carats, which gave it a content of 3.12 grams of pure gold.[22]

Two years later, Florence followed Venice's example. It was the summer of 1530; the Tuscan city had expelled the Medici for the second time and had become a Republic. The continuous state of war had prostrated the economy and in particular the public finances. In June,

> there being some quantity of gold in the mint that it would take a long time to refine,[23] and wishing to help the city, which is in need of great subventions and large amounts of money, because of the continuous and heavy expenditures it incurs, and not wishing to violate in any way or spoil the goodness and purity of the ducato and Florentine gold, but rather to mint another coin not of the usual sort, in

20. Pesce and Felloni, *Monete genovesi*, p. 314. The Genoese gold scudo retained the characteristics indicated in the text until 1527. In 1528 the weight was brought to 3.41 grams and the fineness to 22.25, with a pure gold content of 3.158 grams.

21. Gnecchi and Gnecchi, *Monete di Milano*, p. 105; and *Corpus Nummorum Italicorum*, vol. 5 (Lombardia and Milan), p. 221. According to these works, during the earlier French occupation of Milan by Louis XII (1500–1512), only multiples of the ducat were coined, not écus.

22. Papadopoli, *Monete di Venezia*, vol. 2, pp. 142, 671, doc. 181.

23. The word *partire* in this context means "refine," that is, bring to 24 carats, the fineness of the florin. This fact suggests that much of the

> order to make some profit on it, following the example of another well-managed Italian republic, which, though in lesser difficulties than we, has used similar methods,

it was decided to issue a gold coin called the Florentine scudo, of 3.42 grams, 22.5 carats, and therefore a fine content of around 3.2 grams of pure gold.[24]

There is something rather pathetic about the declaration quoted above: clearly the authorities had the impression that they were doing something reprehensible, and they tried to justify it by proposing captious technical explanations, such as having too little time to refine the gold, and by bringing up "the example of another well-managed Italian republic," clearly alluding to Venice. If Venice has taken the plunge—so goes the basic argument of the Florentine authorities—we who are in far worse financial straits are justified in following in their footsteps. At the same time it was decided to mint *mezi scudi d'argento dorato* (half scudi of gilded silver) on whose metallic content we have no information.[25] The Republican minting of scudi and half scudi remained, however, very limited: about 90 pounds (approximately 30 kilos) of scudi between June and September 1530, and 1,945 pounds (approximately 660 kilos) of half scudi in the same period.[26] It stopped there.

---

gold that, according to the document, flowed into the mint, arrived there in the form of scudi.

24. Bernocchi, *Monete della Repubblica*, vol. 1, pp. 472–73. The weight of each scudo was determined by the rule "that 99 to 99 1/2 pieces must be struck out of one pound of weight." Since the pound corresponded to 339.5 grams, the weight of the Florentine scudo was between 3.41 and 3.43 grams. See table 8, chap. 4, below.

25. Bernocchi, *Monete della Repubblica*, vol. 1, p. 471.

26. See app. 6.

The scudo appeared in large numbers on the market and gradually replaced the fiorino-ducato after the fall of the Republic. The Medici returned to Florence in the person of Duke Alessandro, and on 7 November 1533 a new scudo was issued (see fig. 3). It was inferior to the previous both in weight (3.395 grams) and in fineness (22 carats) with a fine content of 3.12 grams of pure gold.[27] This time the declared reason for the new minting was that "the ducati (that is, the fiorini) issued at the Florentine mint are readily captured by the neighboring mints for their fine content, and such mints with the captured florins produce gold scudi with great profit."[28] This thesis, which essentially puts forward what would later be known as Gresham's law, that is, that bad money (the scudo) drives out good money (the ducato), was taken up also by Benedetto Varchi. In his *Storia* he writes that from the differences in content of the coins, "it followed that fiorini, which were coined in the Florence mint, were immediately taken outside the city or melted down by other neighboring mints and made into scudi."[29]

For Gresham's law to work it was necessary that the two coins (the florin and the scudo) circulate at the same nominal value, or at least that the divergence between their respective nominal values be inferior to the difference in fine content. In August 1531 a law was passed that the Florentine gold scudo was worth 7 lire and the fiorino (by now officially called ducato) 7.5 lire.[30] It is possible that this difference of value was not enough to

27. Bernocchi, *Monete della Repubblica*, vol. 1, p. 482; vol. 3, p. 124. See also table 8 in chap. 4, below.

28. Bernocchi, *Monete della Repubblica*, vol. 1, pp. 481–82.

29. Varchi, *Storia fiorentina*, bk. 14, chap. 6.

30. Bernocchi, *Monete della Repubblica*, vol. 1, pp. 476–77. See also chap. 4, below.

FIG. 3. The gold scudo of Alessandro de' Medici.
O. ALEXANDER · MED · DVX · R · P · FLOREN ·
R. DEI · VIRTVS · EST · NOBIS ·
O∅2.6 3.4g

save the fiorino.[31] It must also have been difficult to keep in circulation two gold coins that were very similar in weight and with a difference in fineness of only 2 carats, which would not easily be perceived by the majority of people. Institutional factors were also at work. Cosimo, in the course of 1537, managed to obtain the consecration and legitimation of his seizure of power, first from the Florentine senate and then from the emperor. Feeling that he at last had the situation firmly in his hand, among other things he ordered the minting of "a coin with his image on it, as Duke Alessandro had done before; moreover, since all the old money of the city had

31. With a content of around 3.5 grams of pure gold, compared with the 3.2 grams of the 1530 scudo, the florin was about 9 percent better than the latter, whereas the florin's exchange rate of 7 1/2 lire was only 7 percent above that of the scudo at 7 lire.

the fleur de lys and St. John on it, [Cosimo] destroyed and turned all the gold into scudi [with his image]."[32]

Thus the scudo, with its multiples and submultiples, became the prevalent gold piece in the Florentine state. The old fiorino, for all practical purposes, gradually disappeared from the scene. A few pieces were coined at the beginning of the forties, with the bust of Duke Cosimo on the obverse, and with the value 8 lire and 7 soldi.[33] It was, however, a limited coining. In 1561 the mint bought 32 fiorini from Giovan Battista de' Servi at the price of 8 lire 12 soldi each to melt down and "gild four large saucers with a stem to hold drinking cups" for the grand duke.[34] In May 1565 the *Depositoria generale* (the ducal treasury) bought nine others, this time paying 9 lire each for them.[35]

While Florence was experiencing the changes we have briefly hinted at, in the rest of the world important events were taking place in the market of precious metals. In Mexico and Peru, the Spaniards discovered rich deposits of gold and above all silver. For more than a century the "flotas de Indias" showered treasures on

32. Segni, *Istorie fiorentine*, bk. 9, p. 358, under the year 1537.

33. Galeotti, *Monete del Granducato di Toscana*, pp. 44, 45, 62; ASF, Zecca, Fiorinaio, c. 189 (18 August 1542) contains a reference to coin gold ducats at 97 1/2 pieces per pound. This corresponds to a weight of 3.48 grams per piece, slightly less than the traditional weight of 3.5 grams. Although 97 1/2 pieces were struck from one pound, 97 1/3 were returned to the merchants who brought metal to the mint. The difference covered the costs of production and the seigniorage. The nominal value of the pieces was established at 8 lire 7 soldi.

34. ASF, Zecca 249, c. 147r. The ordinance of 18 May 1552 (renewed 4 March 1556) forbade the melting down of Florentine gold and silver coins "except the gold ducats to be used by goldsmiths" (ASF, Leggi e Bandi, app. 65).

35. ASF, Depositeria generale 772, under the date 16 May 1565.

Seville: in the first four decades of the century mainly gold and in the second half of the century mainly silver. From about 1560, the market in Europe began to feel a relative scarcity of gold and an extraordinary abundance of silver. There are two explanations for the phenomenon. First, the exchange rate between silver and gold showed a certain stickiness, in part because of the attempt by the monetary authorities to check the increase in the value of gold. Insofar as the official exchange rate lagged behind the relative market prices of the two metals, overvalued silver coins tended to displace gold coins. We shall see that this phenomenon, common to various European markets, became particularly acute in Florence. The impression that gold was becoming increasingly scarce had also another cause.[36] The steady expansion in the volume of international financial transactions that characterized the second half of the sixteenth century brought about a growing demand for gold pieces. Beginning approximately in the fifties, the increase in demand was not matched by a corresponding proportional increase in supply. On one market after another businessmen were consequently forced to effect payments in silver that had traditionally been made in gold. This necessity increased the pressure to mint a heavy silver coin that in one way or another would substitute for the gold scudo.

There was no lack of examples of heavy silver coins approximately equivalent in value to gold coins. In 1486, the archduke Sigmund of Tyrol, made euphoric by the discovery of large silver deposits within his territory, had had a silver coin minted, by the name of guldiner, weighing about 31.9 grams. The counts Schlick, proprietors of the silver mine in Bohemia at St. Joachimstal

36. See Gianelli, "Problemi monetari genovesi."

(Jachymov), had had silver coins called thaler minted from 1519 that weighed about 28.7 grams.[37] In Spain, Charles I had since the 1550s minted pieces of eight (reals de a ocho; see fig. 4) weighing around 30 grams. With his son, Philip II, this "piece of eight" became "la pieza española por antonomasía" and the most common means of payment used in international transactions.[38]

In Italy, the first appearance in circulation of this sort of maxi-silver coin, four or five times heavier than the testone, seems to have occurred in 1551, in Milan, then part of the Spanish empire. A note published by the eighteenth-century antiquarian Filippo Argelati, drawn from documents that have since been lost, tells us that in October 1551 "scudi, half scudi, and quarters of scudi have been made with his majesty's silver arrived from the Indies for the armies." And further, in November of the same year 1551, "scudi, halves, and quarters have been made for the needs of the army, to be sent to the Imperial Ambassador in Genoa."[39]

It is perfectly logical that it should be the Spaniards, in their Milanese dominion, who introduced into Italy the maxi-silver coin of the real de a ocho type as a substitute for the gold scudo. Unfortunately, the fragment of the document quoted by Argelati gives no indication of the numismatic characteristics of the new coin. We suppose that the silver scudo minted in Milan in the 1550s was around 31 or 32 grams at a 958.3/1000 fineness with

37. The fineness of the guldiner was 937.5/1000. That of the thaler was somewhat less.

38. Mateu y Llopis, *Moneda española*, pp. 253, 257. See also Herrera, *El Duro*; and Dasí, *Estudio de los reales*.

39. Argelati, *De monetis Italiae*, vol. 3, p. 36n. These Milanese coinages of 1551 remain rather mysterious since, according to numismatists, no piece from those years has survived.

FIG. 4. Spanish piece of eight (real de a ocho) minted in Potosi, Peru, about 1580.

a content of about 31 grams of pure silver.[40] In the course of time, the Milanese piece took the name of ducatone.

Venice followed Milan's example twelve years later in 1563. The Venetian authorities, having seen that the mint was flooded with such a mass of silver that to dispose of it in the usual form of coins would be a well-nigh impossible task, ordered the minting of a silver coin with the following characteristics: weight 32.896 grams, fineness 948/1000, fine content 31.19 grams, nominal value 6 Venetian lire and 4 soldi.[41]

40. Ibid., and Cipolla, *Mouvements monétaires*, p. 55.

41. The official document that decreed the minting of the new coin explains the circumstances of the measure as follows: "Finding ourselves at present in the mint with a large quantity of silver both of our Lordship's and of others and seeing that it will continue to arrive in the said mint in large quantities, it is necessary that our mint make room for the incoming silver so that merchants will continue to bring silver into this city. They could not do this if we continue to mint only piccioli of 6, 4, and 2 soldi as we do at present. Our managers, however diligent and productive they are, cannot coin

Four years later in 1567, Genoa decreed the coinage of a silver scudo weighing 37.265 grams, fineness 958.3/1000, fine content 35.71, and valued at 4 Genoan lire.[42]

As in the case of the testone and that of the gold scudo, Florence lagged behind, following in the footsteps of Milan, Venice, and Genoa. In the summer of 1563 "the scarcity and dearth of gold scudi that has come to this and all other Italian markets" was recognized in Florence. Considering "the difficulties that traders have in paying of bills of exchange according to the usages thereof and the traditions of the market," it was decided to authorize merchants and money changers to honor bills of exchange in silver coins "of no lesser currency than the giulio" with a maximum premium of 1 percent.[43] Five years later, owing to the persistent scarcity of gold coins, it was finally decided to follow the example of Milan, Venice, and Genoa. The decree that established the new coin has not been found, but in the summer of 1568 a Florentine diarist noted that "in this summer, there being a great scarcity of gold, in place of gold scudi, silver piastre of 7 lire each were coined and in

---

more than the equivalent of 35,000 ducats a month. If we continue like this we must spend the whole year minting only the silver that is in the mint now" (Papadopoli, *Monete di Venezia*, vol. 2, pp. 270, 704, doc. 234).

42. Meroni, *Libri delle uscite delle monete*, p. XVII. When the silver scudo was coined in 1567, the fine content of the gold scudo was modified and reduced to 3.063 grams of pure gold. This alignment was put into practice so that both the gold scudo and the silver scudo would have the same value of 4 lire (pp. XV, 117).

43. Cantini, *Legislazione toscana*, vol. 5, p. 43 (27 August 1563). When the banker paid the bill of exchange in silver coins instead of gold he had to come to an agreement with the client on the exchange rate to be used. Since the official exchange rate undervalued gold coins, the habit of paying an agio in addition was introduced; see chap. 4, below.

FIG. 5. The silver piastra of Cosimo de' Medici.
O. COSMVS · MEDICES · FLOREN · ET ·
SENAR · DVX · II ·
R. · S · IOANNES · · BAPTISTA · 1568 ·
AØ4.0 32.2g

place of the half scudi, silver coins of 3 lire 10 soldi each were coined."[44]

The information is corroborated by the accounts of the mint, in which, on 10 June 1568, a silver coin to the value of 7 lire is mentioned for the first time.[45] The new coin had not yet been officially christened, and the scrivener of the mint invented the term testone di lire sette (testoon of 7 lire);[46] but soon it was designated ducato d'argento or scudo d'argento or piastra or even piastrone (see fig. 5 and table 3). The money weighed

44. Orsini, *Storia delle monete*, pp. 11–12.

45. ASF, Zecca 120, under 10 June 1568. The information given by Boissin ("Risposta," chap. 15, p. 119, col. 1) in *De monetis Italiae*, ed. Argelati, that piastre of 7 lire were already coined under Cosimo, and that samples from 1551 and 1561 were to be found in circulation, is unreliable.

46. ASF, Zecca 120, c. 94, under the date 21 June 1568.

TABLE 3. The intrinsic characteristics of the first gold scudi and the first silver piastre coined in the principal mints of northern Italy.

	Weight (gm) (*a*)	Fineness (x/24 for gold; x/1000 for silver) (*b*)	Fine metal content (gm) (c) = $a \cdot b$
Gold scudi			
Genoa, 1508	3.43	22.5	3.22
1528	3.41	22.25	3.16
Milan, c. 1520	3.50	22	3.21
Venice, 1528	3.40	22	3.12
Florence, 1530	3.42	22.5	3.21
Florence, 1533	3.40	22	3.12
Silver piastre			
Milan, 1551	31–32(?)	958.3(?)	30–31(?)
Venice, 1563	32.90	948	31.19
Genoa, 1567	37.27	958.3	35.71
Florence, 1568	32.56	958.3	31.20

32.5–32.6 grams, at the traditional fineness of 958.333/1000, and had therefore a content of around 31.20 grams of pure silver.[47]

With the coining of the silver piastre in 1568 the Florentine system of metallic currency acquired a structure that was destined to last unchanged until the end of

47. ASF, Zecca 154–55, 157, 161, and Fiorinaio, cc. 191–92.

the century and beyond. This structure was accurately described by an author of the time, Giuliano de' Ricci, whose testimony we will often refer to in chapter 6. Giuliano had literary pretensions, which were largely unjustified, and to earn his living he had, to his chagrin, to practice trade. He had, therefore, in spite of himself, firsthand knowledge of monetary affairs. In his *Cronaca*, under the year 1571, he described the Florentine monetary system in the following terms:

> And so that it may be seen which and how many sorts of money and of what fineness and weight are minted in Florence today, I make a note of it here below.

	Lira	Soldo	Denero
The piastrone, or silver ducato	7	–	–
The half silver ducato	3	10	–
The riccio,[48] that is the testone	2	–	–
The cosimo, that is the lira	1	–	–
The giulio; 2/3 of a lira and 3 giulii make a riccio	–	13	4

All the coins above are of the same fineness of 11 ounces 12 denari

The crazia is worth five quattrini; it is of worse fineness and there are 12 in a lira	–	1	8

48. The coin was called *riccio* ("curl"), for the duke's curly hair.

The quattrino of which there are three in a soldo	–	–	4
The gold scudo of 70 grains of the ducal mint	7	12	–
The gold scudo of other mints	7	10	–

This list is a perfect fit with the data and information given above in this chapter.[49] So far the discourse has been of a numismatic rather than an economic nature, but it provides the economic historian with some clues. The main innovations in the Italian currency system between the end of the fifteenth century and the end of the sixteenth were taken up in Florence rather late, and the Florentine market showed repeatedly, first with the testone, then with the scudo, and finally with the piastre, that it had lost its leadership in the monetary field, not only in Europe as a whole but even in Italy, and that it followed rather than led innovation. Looking at it from another point of view, we can say that in the course of the sixteenth century a strong conservative tendency prevailed in Florentine monetary policy and, as we shall see in the following chapters, reached its acme during the reign of Francesco de' Medici.

49. See app. 1 for a more detailed analysis of the Ricci text.

CHAPTER TWO

The Money of Account

IN GIULIANO de' Ricci's list of Florentine coins, the nominal value of each individual type is expressed, as was common at the time, in units of account of the lira-soldo-denaro system. This system, the traditional one dating back to the Carolingian monetary reforms of the eighth century, was enhanced in Florence in the first half of the sixteenth century by a new unit of account.

Between 1502 and 1530, that is, for almost thirty years, the exchange rate of the gold florin remained stable at 7 lire. After 1530, owing to the devaluation of the silver currency in that and the following year, the rate of exchange of the florin had risen and the florin itself had gradually become rarer, being progressively replaced, as we have seen in chapter 1, by the scudo. In bookkeeping practice however, the habit of counting in units of 7 lire had been established: in other words, especially when the accounting of substantial transactions were involved, the utility of a multiple of the lira had been clearly demonstrated. Thus, after 1530, the florin of 7 lire was used as an abstract unit of account with no relation to the real gold florin, which circulated at a higher exchange rate, was increasingly known as the ducato, and was rapidly becoming extinct in any case.

Consequently, after 1530 the traditional accounting

system was the following (henceforth referred to as system A):

System A

1 fiorino a moneta	= 7 lire	= 140 soldi	= 1,680 denari piccioli
	1 lira	= 20 soldi	= 240 denari piccioli
		1 soldo	= 12 denari piccioli

This system of accounting was called "a moneta" in contemporary documents and the term "a moneta" was normally placed next to the word fiorino; after the word and the figure indicating the sum of denari, it was normally specified that these were piccioli (that is, the real coins named denari piccioli).

One variation of the A system was the so-called system of the fiorino d'oro di moneta, which was organized as follows:[1]

System B

1 gold fiorino di moneta	= 7 lire of denari piccioli	= 1,680 denari piccioli
	= 20 soldi	= 240 denari
	1 soldo	= 12 denari

Despite the florin's being described as "fiorino d'oro" (gold florin), after 1530 it too was a purely abstract bookkeeping unit. By definition it was equal to 7 lire of denari piccioli and was therefore identical to the fiorino a

1. One must note the small but substantial difference between the expression "di moneta" of the B system of accounts and the expression "a moneta" of the A system. The distinction should not

moneta of the A system. However, it was subdivided directly into 20 soldi and 12 denari instead of having the lira as a submultiple, and the soldi and the denari as submultiples of the lira. Consequently, while the florin of the B system was the same as the florin of the A system, the soldo of system B was the equivalent of 7 soldi of system A and correspondingly the denaro of system B (which was not denaro picciolo but represented ideally the 240th part of the florin di moneta) was equivalent to 7 denari of the A system, that is, 7 denari piccioli. The soldo and the denaro of system B, as well as the florin, were abstract units of account and the linkage to effective coins took place through equivalence: 1 fiorino = 7 lire of piccioli = 1,680 denari piccioli (where the only effective piece of money was the denaro picciolo).

Because the piastra, also known as the silver ducato, had maintained the same value of 7 lire from its debut in 1568 until the end of the century and beyond, in bookkeeping practice the term ducato was occasionally substituted for that of florin in both system A and system B. In other words, in the last three decades of the sixteenth century, in bookkeeping terms, florin and ducato were both used to indicate 7 lire.

As we shall see in chapter 4, around 1538 the official value of the real gold scudo rose to 7 1/2 lire (that is, 7 lire and 10 soldi). But this rate did not remain stable in the long run, despite the fact that the duke had got it into his head to impose it on the market at all costs.[2] The rise in value of the scudo was due principally to the progressive depreciation of silver in relation to gold. In

---

be taken as absolute. I have noticed that some accountants used the expression "di moneta" to indicate the system that others more appropriately called "a moneta."

2. In 1556, however, the duke ordered that the Florentine gold scudo be exchanged at a rate of 7 lire 12 soldi. See chap. 4, below.

the meantime, however, the scudo of 7 1/2 lire had become part of bookkeeping practice—especially among those who dealt in bills of exchange, such as bankers and money changers—so that another system of account came into being:

System C

1 gold scudo =	7 lire 10 soldi	=	1,800 denari piccioli	
=	20 soldi	=	240 denari	
	1 soldo	=	12 denari	

The soldo and the denaro of this system were equal, respectively, to 7 1/2 soldi and 7 1/2 denari of the A system of account.[3] Both the soldo and the denaro and, from an uncertain date around 1555, the gold scudo itself, valued at 7 1/2 lire in the C system, were mere bookkeeping units of account that did not correspond to real coins.[4] Giovan Battista della Torre says this clearly in his *Ragguaglio di Piazze*, where, at the end of the century, he correctly comments:

> this scudo of ours [of 7 1/2 lire] should be that which this mint issues . . . but the increase in the quantity of silver has caused the above increase [in the value of gold], so that in this market [Florence], this scudo remains an imaginary [unit of account].

3. Within the C system itself the soldo of the equivalence 1 scudo = 7 lire 10 soldi is not the same thing as the soldo of the equivalence 1 scudo = 20 soldi; the second is worth seven and a half times the first. This is because the soldo of the equivalence 1 scudo = 7 lire 10 soldi is 1/20 of the lira, while the soldo of the equivalence 1 scudo = 20 soldi is 1/20 of the scudo.

4. The linkage of the imaginary scudo of 7 1/2 lire and its imaginary submultiples with real coins came about through the equivalence 1 scudo = 1,800 denari piccioli, where denari piccioli were real metallic coins.

> The principal merchants and in particular the money changers keep their books in this sort of scudo. Shopkeepers and artisans keep them in ducati, or should we say fiorini, with the value of 7 lire each.[5]

Thus Florentine businessmen used different unit-of-account systems: in the second half of the century the most important merchants, bankers, and money changers kept their books mainly in the units of system C, in which the scudo was worth 7 1/2 lire, whereas the shopkeepers and artisans kept their books in fiorino of 7 lire (and its submultiples) of the systems I have called A and B.[6] In practice, however, things were even more complicated, since the same bookkeeper could use different units of account in the same book. In the register of the mint preserved in the Florentine State Archive in case 150, for example, on the same line of the same page, with reference to the same transaction, the value of issues is expressed in units of account of system A, while the value of the so-called *fievolezza* is expressed in units of system B.

The systems of account described above are by no means exhaustive. Bookkeepers satisfied their every

5. Della Torre, "Ragguaglio di Piazze," in ASF, Depositeria 425. See also Peri, *Negotiante*, pt. 2, relazione 4: in Florence "bookkeeping is held in scudi, known as gold scudi, which are valued at 7 lire 10 soldi and are imaginary. These scudi have their submultiples, which are added in 20 and in 12: that is, 20 soldi are a scudo and 12 denari a soldo."

6. The fact that bankers and money changers used system C is to be linked to the fact that bills of exchange were traditionally denominated and settled in gold coins and specifically, after 1540, in gold scudi. It must be noted that of the three systems of account most commonly used on the Florentine market during the sixteenth century, none used gold as its backing money: all three rested on biglione coins.

whim by inventing their own units of account. In Colle Val d'Elsa they counted in florins of 4 lire 4 soldi; in Borgo San Sepolcro in florins of 4 lire and in florins of 3 lire 10 soldi; in Arezzo in florins of 4 lire 5 soldi.[7] Furthermore, bookkeepers of important state or semipublic offices might have their own systems, so that for collection of tithes, tithe florins were used, and in the *Riformagioni* so-called *fiorini di Camera* were used. "As far as the Monte [Comune] florins are concerned, they are of a different kind depending on the place they are entered up."[8]

All this created a great deal of confusion, which the modern scholar finds difficult to disentangle, and in which contemporaries kept their bearings only with the greatest difficulty.[9] At the end of the seventeenth century, the grand duke's administration, overwhelmed by such chaos, asked Claudio Boissin, chancellor of the Monte Comune of Florence, to prepare a report that was intended to clarify the meaning of the various types of florins of account in use in Tuscany. Boissin set to work with the best will in the world, but, in part because the matter in itself was too intricate, and in part because he was something of a muddler, he drew up a report that, although full of data (not always reliable), is anything but clarifying.[10]

7. Boissin, "Risposta," in *De monetis Italiae*, ed. Argelati, vol. 4, p. 109, chap. 12. Giorgio Vasari in his will of May 1568 left two legacies, expressed in florins of 4 lire 5 soldi (Gaye, *Carteggio inedito*, pp. 506, 507, 513).

8. Boissin, "Risposta," in *De monetis Italiae*, ed. Argelati, vol. 4, p. 123, chap. 16.

9. As Lane and Mueller (*Money and Banking*, p. 490) have written of Venetian coins, while the real metallic money system was relatively simple in structure, the accounting system grafted onto it was extraordinarily complex.

10. Boissin's report was published in *De monetis Italiae*, ed. Argelati, vol. 4. A manuscript copy of the original is to be found in ASF, Manoscritti, 766.

This state of affairs had its roots in the distant past. The reasons for confusion were at the same time simple and complicated. In Carolingian times the abstract units of account, lira and soldo, were introduced to alleviate the problems caused by the fact that there was only one denomination in circulation, the denaro with a content 1.67 of pure silver, which had no effective multiples. After the twelfth century, silver pieces were coined which were heavier than the denaro and from the middle of the thirteenth century gold coins were minted. The monetary authorities, however, did not succeed in keeping the exchange rates steady among the various denominations (especially between gold coins and silver and biglione coins); in other words, several denominations circulated but did not form an integrated system of multiples and submultiples. The experience of those centuries shows that if, at the level of means of payment, coins tied to each other by fixed rates can be done away with, at an accounting level multiples and submultiples must be linked by stable rates.[11]

Any kind of accounting system had to have the backing of a real coin from which to derive its values: that is to say, it had to be anchored with a fixed rate to at least one real coin. If the coins in circulation were correctly aligned as regards their fine, or pure metal, content, there were no problems. If the alignment did not exist, however, or if it came unstuck, a version of Gresham's law went into effect by which bad money drove out good as backing money of the accounting system. This fact was the root of the paradox that characterized the monetary affairs of the time: the petty biglione coins had a disruptive influence on the monetary system quite out of proportion to their economic weight. These coins had

11. Cipolla, *Moneta e civiltà*, chap. 4.

proportionately much higher production costs because of their relatively light weight (that is to say, from one unit of weight a larger number of pieces were produced compared with heavier coins), so that they were never aligned as regards fine content with coins of greater unitary value, and they circulated at a nominal value appreciably higher (by 10 or 20 percent) than the value of their metal content. If these petty biglione coins were further debased or issued in excessive quantities, three possibilities were left for the large silver coins: either their intrinsic value was debased proportionately; or they were revalued, that is, their rate of exchange was raised; or they were destined to disappear. Whatever the solution, the exchange rate between the weaker money and the unit of account remained fixed, thus dragging the latter downward too.

In sixteenth-century Milan, for example, the authorities did not know how to prevent the debasement of the petty biglione coins or how to control the volume of their issue so that the silver ducatone (which was the Milanese equivalent of the Florentine piastra) and the other large silver coins continued to grow in value. Florence, however, from the middle of the century, practiced, as we shall see, a severely restrictive policy for petty coins—that is, crazie, quattrini, and denari—limiting their debasement and above all blocking the volume in circulation. Thus the Florentine authorities managed to neutralize the destabilizing effect of the biglione and prevented it from dragging the unit of account in its wake.[12] This led to such a degree of stability in the value of large silver coins—piastre, testoni, lire, and giulii—in terms of the money of account, that it gave the erroneous

12. See, e.g., Montanari, "Zecca" pp. 356–57.

impression that the latter was anchored to those same silver coins.

The stabilization of the exchange rate of gold coins was, however, not achieved despite the stubborn insistence of the grand duke. As we have seen above, it was the successive increases in the value of the gold fiorino initially, and later the gold scudo, that gave birth to the new Florentine units of account of the sixteenth century.

CHAPTER THREE

Silver Coins and the Silver Parity of the Lira

THE VALUE of the unit of account depended on the exchange value of the metallic support money. In turn, the exchange value of any coin depended, though to a different degree, on its content of metal. The available sources for establishing the metallic content of the coins in circulation at that time are (*a*) surviving specimens in numismatic collections, (*b*) minting orders, and (*c*) the mint accounts. In the case of the large silver coins, the value of their silver content represented 97–98 percent of their nominal exchange value.[1] In the case of the biglione coins (crazie, quattrini, and denari piccioli), the ratio was lower, owing to the much higher incidence of seigniorage and production costs. Thus, for example, in the 1540s and 1550s the nominal value of crazie and quattrini could be broken down approximately as follows:[2]

1. The mint accounts always indicate the difference between the nominal value of the coins minted and price paid by the mint for the metal. This difference, which includes the costs of production (*brassaggio*) and the mint profits (*signoraggio*), was usually around 2 or 3 percent for silver coins.

2. ASF, Zecca 150.

	Crazie	Quattrini
Pure silver	90%	75%
Copper	1%	5%
Mintage and seigniorage	9%	20%

Both Orsini in 1756 and Galeotti in 1930, in their works devoted to the coins of the grand duchy, for the most part used sources *a* and *b*.[3] The problem, when source *a* is used, is represented by the different states of conservation of the surviving coins. To take care of this problem, modern numismatists use the statistical technique of frequency tables. Neither Galeotti in 1930 nor Orsini in 1756 used this technique; however, by integrating the analysis of the coins with the study of source *b*, that is, the minting orders, Orsini, and more especially Galeotti, achieved results that are substantially valid. The pages that follow are based on sources *b* and *c*, that is, minting orders and mint accounts, and take into consideration as a form of control the conclusions numismatists have come to in their analyses of the surviving specimens.

Two fundamental types of information can be gleaned from the years for which the mint accounts have survived. One refers to single transactions carried out by individuals with the mint; the other deals with the macro data of the minting activity. From the first type of annotation we learn that from a given quantity of metal brought to the mint by an individual, a given quantity of coins was obtained. From the second type of record we

3. Orsini, *Storia delle monete*; Galeotti, *Monete del Granducato di Toscana*. In order to establish the parity of the Florentine money in the sixteenth century, Parenti (*Prime ricerche*, pp. 50–58) has relied for the most part on the results of Orsini and Galeotti, and Carli, *Delle monete*.

learn that in the course of a semester (which usually ran from the first of March to the end of August and from the first of September to the last day of February), the mint, having received a total amount X of metal, produced the total amount *Y* of money, out of which it paid the sum Z to the proprietors of the metal and retained for itself the amount (*Y* − *Z*) to cover the costs of production and the seigniorage.

In several single transactions, a certain amount of money in various denominations (piastre, testoni, cosimi, giulii) was obtained, probably according to the specific orders of an individual. These cases were, however, relatively rare. More frequent were those in which a single type of coin was struck at the request of the private citizen and delivered to the same citizen. When and if this situation occurred, it is possible to calculate the average weight of the coins in question.[4] These averages refer to the single amounts delivered to individuals and called at that time *sorte*. Owing to the deficient technology of the day it was not possible to mint coins that were identical in weight to a hundredth of a gram, so that the averages of the *sorte* show variations that are not negligible. In October 1576, for example, one *sorte* of testoons gives the average weight of 9.2674 grams, two other *sorte* give an average weight of 9.2995 grams, and yet another gives an average weight of 9.2877 grams.[5] In

4. The mint books for 13 October 1576, for example, tell us that from a *sorte* of 23 1/2 pounds of popolino silver, 215.1 *mane* of testoons were coined. Since *mane* meant four units, it follows that from 23 1/2 pounds (7979 grams) of popolino silver (958.33/1000), 861 (215 × 4 + 1) testoons were extracted, at an average weight per testoon of 9.27 grams of popolino silver, that is, an average content of 8.88 grams of pure silver (1000/1000) per testoon. See ASF, Zecca 155.

5. Ibid.

addition, in the course of the century, the authorities discovered that the scales used by the mint were not precise and falsified weighings.[6] Under these conditions it is obviously senseless to indicate the weight of coins and the fine content in figures with more than one or two decimal points.

Table 4 shows the contents of pure silver (1000/1000) of the various coins. The data in question derive from both minting orders and mint accounts: the two sets of data match and fit in well with the conclusions drawn by Orsini and Galeotti through numismatical analysis. On the basis of the data in table 4, a further elaboration has yielded the data in table 5, in which the grams of pure silver (1000/1000) are indicated, equivalent to 1 lira (unit of account) when the lira was paid with different types of coins. This elaboration aims at establishing the degree of alignment of the various denominations. A superficial glance at the data in table 5 will suffice to show that the various silver coins were correctly aligned among themselves, in the sense that whatever the specie in which a debt was paid, the creditor received the same amount of pure silver per lira. The alignment was broken at the level of the half giulio and the biglione coins (crazie and quattrini), whose minting costs were higher in proportion to their nominal value. It was the metallic weakness of these petty coins that, as we have already mentioned, made them the Achilles' heel of the monetary system and caused the authorities to limit the status of these

6. See the auditors' report of 2 July 1571, quoted below. On 25 February 1573 the authorities had "the weights both of the control office and of the mint adjusted, having found that the former underweighed the silver it received 14 denari for every 50 pounds, while the weights of the mint were short 42 1/2 denari out of every 50 pounds" (ASF, Zecca 153).

TABLE 4. Pure silver (1000/1000) content expressed in grams of the various denominations of silver and biglione coins minted in Florence in the sixteenth century.

Year	Type of source*	Piastra (= 7 lire)	Testone (= 2 lire)	Cosimo (= 1 lira)	Giulio**	Mezzo giulio	Grossone**	Crazia (= 20 denari)	Quattrino (= 4 denari)
1503	d						1.91		
1504	d				3.37				
1506	d						1.88		
1509	d								0.07
1510	d						1.88		
1531	d				3.30		1.79		
1533	d								0.07
1535	d				3.21				0.06
1538	d				3.08			0.36	0.06
1539	d			4.60					
1540–49	z		9.21	4.60	3.07			0.35	0.06
1550	z				3.05			0.35	

1552	z				3.02			0.35	
1559–60	z							0.33	0.06
1561	z		8.92						
1565	z		8.86						
1568	z	31.20			2.95				
1571	d				2.97				
1576	z	31.17	8.90			1.45			
1577	z	31.23	8.90			1.45			
1578	z	31.23	8.88			1.45			
1581	z			4.45					
1582	z	31.24							
1583	z			4.46					
1597	d	31.20	8.91	4.46	2.97	1.49			

NOTE: Small variations such as those for the silver piastra are to be ascribed to imperfect minting and measuring techniques. The piastra, for example, kept to all intents and purposes the same silver content. This is true for the testone from 1571.

* d = decreto; z = mint accounts.

** In 1504 the giulio was worth 12 soldi 6 denari. In 1530–31 the value of the giulio was raised to 13 soldi 4 denari (see chap. 1). At the same time, the grossone was brought from 7 soldi to 7 soldi 6 denari.

TABLE 5. The parity of the Florentine lira in grams of pure silver (1000/1000) when paid in various coins.

Year	Piastra (= 7 lire)	Testone (= 2 lire)	Cosimo (= 1 lira)	Giulio*	Mezzo giulio	Grossone*	Crazia (= 20 denari)	Quattrino (= 4 denari)
1503						5.4		
1504				5.4				
1506						5.4		
1509								4.2
1510						5.4		
1531				4.9		4.8		
1533								4.2
1535				4.8				3.7
1538				4.6			4.3	3.6
1539			4.6					
1540–49		4.6	4.6	4.6			4.2	3.6

1550				4.6			4.2	
1552				4.5			4.2	
1559–60							4.0	3.4
1561		4.5						
1565		4.4						
1568	4.5			4.4				
1571				4.5				
1576	4.4	4.5			4.3			
1577	4.5	4.5			4.3			
1578	4.5	4.4			4.3			
1581			4.5					
1582	4.5							
1583			4.5					
1597	4.5	4.5	4.5	4.5	4.5			

NOTE: Discrepancies between these data and those of table 4 are due to the rounding of figures.

* In 1504 the giulio was worth 12 soldi 6 denari. In 1530–31 the value of the giulio was brought to 13 soldi 4 denari (see chap. 1) and the value of the grossone was brought from 7 soldi to 7 soldi 6 denari.

coins as legal tender to payments of limited amounts.[7]

In order to analyze the variations in the metallic content of silver coins over time, from 1543 onward, the gaps in the data in tables 4 and 5 that deal with the single types of coin can be filled in with the data from table A4 referring to the entire volume and value of metallic money issued in the various six-month periods from the total amount of metal delivered to the mint. This further series of data has the advantage of greater continuity and greater sensitivity to progressive debasement.[8] By fitting together the various pieces of available data, we gain a reasonably clear picture of what happened.

Despite the severe political, military, economic and social adversities of the first three decades of the sixteenth century, the monetary authorities were able to contain the debasement of silver and biglione coins within very tight margins. As table 6 shows, in the first decade of the century the stages of monetary debasement are datable at 1503, 1504, 1506, and 1510.

Table 6 differs from tables 4 and 5 in that it includes the quinto di scudo, excluded from the earlier tables on account of its exceptionally brief life. Moreover, in table 6 the content of the single coins and the metallic parity of the lira are calculated, respectively, to a thousandth and a hundredth of a gram in order to highlight the stages of a devaluation that, as we have already mentioned, was kept within very narrow limits. Despite the

7. The ordinances, for example, prohibited the payment of bills of exchange, or of sums of a certain entity to be made in denominations of less than the giulio.

8. The figures in tables 4 and 5 have been rounded to the nearest decimal point, and in several cases this rounding masks the slight and gradual changes in the debasement of the single species.

TABLE 6. Pure silver (1000/1000) content of Florentine silver coins and corresponding silver parity of the Florentine lira di piccioli, 1503–10.

	Content in gm of pure AR			Silver parity of the lira in gm of pure AR on the basis of silver content and nominal value		
Year	Quinto di scudo	Giulio	Grosso	Quinto di scudo	Giulio	Grosso
1503	7.398		1.907	5.28		5.44
1504		3.367			5.38	
1506			1.881			5.37
1510			1.875			5.36

SOURCE: The data in the table are drawn from information provided by Bernocchio, *Monete della Repubblica*, vols. 1, 3. The nominal values of the three coins in the years covered in the table are as follows: 1 quinto di scudo = 1 lira 8 soldi; 1 giulio = 12 soldi 6 denari; and 1 grosso = 7 soldi.

fact that the touching up was done at four distinct intervals, the depreciation over the whole of the decade was altogether only 1.5 percent. In the two following decades, from 1511 to 1529, stability prevailed. It should not come as a surprise, therefore, that silver and biglione coins held their own against gold coins for the whole of the three decades and the exchange rate of the gold florin remained stable at 7 lire of piccioli.[9]

9. Bernocchi, *Monete della Repubblica*, vol. 3, p. 88.

The slide began during the thirties and took place in four stages. The first devaluation occurred during the summer of 1530. Florence was at war; the imperial troops had besieged the city from the preceding October; famine, plague, and the specter of a sacking like the one Rome had succumbed to three years previously haunted the city; the state coffers were empty. Devaluation became an unpleasant but unavoidable necessity. Given the exceptional circumstances, the devaluation was also conducted in an unusual way by Florentine standards. The Florentine mint traditionally coined on commission for third parties and the only profits due to the comune from devaluation were indirect and derived from the coinage tax known as seigniorage: in other words, devaluation served as an incentive for the flow of metal to the mint and thus helped to inflate seigniorage. In June 1530, it was decided that the new coinage was to be exclusively for the comune, so that the municipality could keep to itself all the profits deriving from the maneuver. However, even in a situation of extreme emergency, the principle that had traditionally prevailed in Florence was adhered to, namely, that any debasement in silver coins should be in weight alone. The fineness was not to be modified, since it represented a parameter the public found difficult to evaluate. It is worth repeating these concepts in the words of the legislation of the time:

> Considered, that it is necessary to help the city as far as money is concerned as much as possible and by all possible means, the treasury being empty by continued expenditures, and not wanting because of this to deteriorate in any way the fineness of Florentine silver, which up to now has been preserved intact, but soon to operate on the weight to the benefit of the Comune of Florence,

> . . . it seeming appropriate that what is done by such a republic should be done in such a way that everyone can see that they are not being defrauded in some guise, as happens when the fineness is lowered, since many people are not aware of it.[10]

On these grounds, which showed how deeply rooted was the tradition of monetary transparency in Florence, a debasement of the various silver coins was ordered. Instead of the 8 florins, 12 soldi, 6 denari (60 lire 7 soldi 6 denari) that had previously been minted from a pound of silver of popolino fineness, it was ordered that the equivalent of 8 florins, 17 soldi, 6 denari (62 lire 1 soldo 6 denari) be produced. This meant a reduction in the silver parity of the lira of almost 3 percent, from 5.39 grams of pure silver to 5.24. This however did not suffice. The following year, 1531, a new devaluation became necessary: this time it was decided to leave the metallic content of the various coins intact and increase their nominal values. The new devaluation was rather drastic. Calculated on the basis of the giulio, whose nominal value changed from 12 soldi 6 denari to 13 soldi 4 denari, while its weight and fineness remained the same, the devaluation of the Florentine lira was over 6 percent. Between 1530 and 1531, therefore, the silver parity of the lira lost almost 10 percent. Following this depreciation, the exchange rate of the gold florin, which in the preceding decades had remained at 7 lire, began to rise.

The Medici had meanwhile consolidated their power in the person of Alessandro. In March 1535, as was mentioned in chapter 1, he issued a general decree aimed at

10. Ibid., vol. 1, pp. 471–72.

reorganizing the whole monetary and payment system and making the carlino-barile-giulio the kingpin of the monetary system. On this occasion the content of the coin was slightly reduced, to 3.21 grams of pure silver (see table 2), so that the parity of the lira, with reference to the giulio, went from 4.9 grams to 4.8 grams. In the meantime there was an attempt to limit the quantity of biglione coins in circulation by ordering that "for the future, no more grossi or crazie or black quattrini shall be minted under any circumstances, except black quattrini, of which some may be struck for an amount that will be explicitly decided by the Officials of the Monte and the Masters of the Mint for the times concerned."[11]

Thus an attempt was made to enforce good monetary management on the basis of three points that mutually reinforced one another: (1) stability and correct alignment of the various silver coins; (2) strict control of the quantity of petty coins in circulation; (3) elimination, as much as possible and with few exceptions, of foreign coins from internal circulation. These were the objectives, at least, and they were applied effectively only in the very long run. In the short run, good intentions remained on paper. As far as the first point is concerned, in November 1538 the content of the giulio was lowered from 3.21 grams of pure silver, as had been established in 1535, to 3.08 grams (see table 2), a devaluation therefore of almost 4 percent.[12] On the second point, the decree suspending the minting of grossi, crazie, and black quattrini went unheeded at least insofar as the crazie were concerned. In fact, already in November

11. ASF, Zecca, Fiorinaio, cc. 184v–185r. The passage is incorrectly reproduced by Cantini, *Legislazione toscana*, vol. 1, p. 85.

12. The reason given for the debasement of the giulio was that "nowadays in the city of Florence and its domain no silver coins are

1538 it was decreed, and later confirmed in 1542, that crazie could be coined with a 4 ounce per pound fineness (333.3/1000) at the rate of 318 pieces per pound, that is, around 1.1 grams in weight and a content of 0.36 grams of pure silver.[13] The mint registers show that crazie, quattrini, and piccioli continued to be coined, especially in the first half of the 1540s.[14] Some progress was made on the third point although the text of the 1538 decree itself, which ordered the reduction of the metallic content of the giulio, hinted at the continued presence of coins "of other mints" on the Florentine market, which together with worn Florentine coins played the role of "bad money."

We have just seen that after three decades of stability, the silver currency was debased in four stages, in 1530, 1531, 1535, and 1538. In the 1540s, stability once more asserted itself. The mint registers, which provide data on the value and volume of the output from 1543 onward, show that from 1543 to 1548 the silver money was kept stable at 70 1/2 lira per pound of popolino

---

available for everyday use, and those that are available, both Florentine and from other mints, are mostly worn and underweight" (ASF, Zecca, Fiorinaio, c. 188v). Since the nominal value of the giulio was 13 soldi 4 denari, minting 105.5 pieces for every pound of alloy meant producing coins for the amount of 70.33 lire for every pound of popolino silver.

13. ASF, Zecca, Fiorinaio, cc. 191–92 (the retrospective part of the report of 1 March 1597 is given in app. 3).

14. ASF, Zecca 150; also 116–119, 166, 191, 209. A contemporary chronicle (ASF, Bardi, sez. 3, n. 14) provides the following information: "February 1545: certain whimsical people approached the Duke about money. . . . They were saying to Cosimo that for the common good it would be a wise thing to issue piccioli: in this whimsical fashion and to the detriment of the poor, 15 or 16 thousand scudi worth of piccioli were coined with the coat of arms of the Medici." For the actual coinages of petty coins in those years see app. 7.

silver (see app. 7, table A4, col. *c*), which meant a silver parity for the lira of 4.6 grams.[15] From 1548 to 1565, a long phase of creeping depreciation was experienced once again. The regulations of November 1538 were still in force, but the mint extracted an increasingly greater quantity of money from each pound of popolino silver. The subphases of this creeping devaluation can be summarized schematically as follows (the progressively higher number of lire and tenths of a lira extracted from a pound of popolino silver is indicated in parentheses):

1543–48:	stability
1548–52:	devaluation (from 70.5 to 71.8 lire)
1552–55:	stability
1555–62:	devaluation (from 71.8 to 72.8 lire)
1562–64:	stability
1565:	devaluation (from 72.8 to 73.5 lire)

As we shall see, the ducal auditors found that the mint accounts were not kept correctly and that already toward the end of 1562 the mint was extracting around 73.5 lire of silver coins from a pound of popolino silver.[16] If so, the devaluation dated at 1565 above may be due not to a real depreciation of the currency in that year but to more careful bookkeeping practice. At any rate, 73.5 lire per pound of popolino meant for the lira a parity of 4.4 grams of pure silver. Compared with the 4.6 grams at

15. I show here the method used to estimate the parity of the lira. From a pound of popolino silver a total of 70 1/2 lire in silver coins were extracted. A pound (339.5 grams) of popolino silver (958.33/1000) contained 325.35 grams of pure silver (1000/1000). Thus, if from 325.35 grams of pure silver coins for a total of 70 1/2 lire were minted, it follows that one lira corresponded to 4.6 grams of pure silver.

16. See the text below at n. 24.

the beginning of the 1540s, the new parity meant a debasement of about 4 percent throughout the whole of the twenty-year period. It was a trifling devaluation, but it was disturbing in the sense that it had never been legally authorized.

It is not at all clear whether or to what extent the duke and the monetary authorities approved of the slide of silver coins between 1548 and 1565. What is definitely clear is that something changed during the 1560s, and the change inaugurated an era of strict conservative monetary policy. In all likelihood this "something" was the rise of Francesco de' Medici, whose father, Cosimo, on his abdication on 1 May 1564, established him as the effective head of the government.[17] Francesco's conservative, meticulous, and authoritarian character has been widely discussed by historians, and events in the monetary field tie in well with these traits of his personality. On the whole, what happened between 1564 and 1571 was the meticulous and authoritarian implementation of the monetary rules that had been intimated in the decree of March 1535 but had never fully been put into practice.

It began with the petty coins. It must be remembered that the decree of March 1535 suspended the issuing of crazie and grossi and limited the issuing of quattrini. Subsequent decrees in 1538 and 1542 contradicted the ban of 1535, and the mint records show that crazie and quattrini continued to be minted until the summer of 1563.[18] Worse still, especially in the years between 1557 and 1560, crazie and quattrini were issued at much lower fineness than that stipulated by the decrees in force at

17. See Galluzzi, *Istoria del Granducato di Toscana*, vol. 2, p. 279; and Diaz, *Granducato*, p. 232.

18. See app. 7, table A5.

the time. In fact, although the decrees of 1538 and 1542 prescribed crazie with a 333.3/1000 fineness and weighing 1.068 grams, between 1557 and 1562 crazie were coined with a fineness of 319.4 and weighing between 1.035 and 1.014 grams apiece. The same was true for quattrini: although the 1538 regulations envisaged a fineness of 83.3/1000, in actual fact, around 1560, quattrini were struck with a fineness of 76.39/1000.[19]

During 1563, someone highly placed decided that the time had come to put an end to this state of affairs and to stop, once and for all, the minting of crazie and quattrini. The tone of the ordinance of August 1563 was peremptory: "That in future it is in no way allowed to coin either crazie or quattrini, without the permission of the Lords and his Illustrious Excellency (the Grand Duke) in his mint in Florence." To avoid the mint master's having the least temptation to infringe the ban, the ordinance laid down "that all the dies with which the said crazie and quattrini are struck must be put in a chest and locked with two keys, one of which is to be kept by the Magistrate of the Lords and the other by the Lords of the mint."[20]

A lugubrious hint at the "death penalty" awaiting any infraction gave the final touch to this decree.[21] The mint accounts show clearly that this ordinance was immediately and scrupulously respected.[22]

While this was going on another problem was coming to a head. The mint was usually managed for a period of

19. ASF, Zecca, Fiorinaio, cc. 191–92 (retrospective report of 1 March 1597, reproduced in app. 3). The data in this report are corroborated by the mint accounts for the years 1559–60 (ASF, Zecca 151).

20. Cantini, *Legislazione toscana*, vol. 5, p. 40 (6 August 1563).

21. Galeotti, *Le monete del Granducato di Toscana*, p. 55.

22. See app. 7, table A5.

thirty months at a time, renewable on expiration, by a so-called *provveditore di zecca* (mint supervisor).[23] At the end of August 1560 a certain Bernardo Baldini took over the management. He had held the post previously and it was renewed for thirty months, up to the end of February 1563. As usual, during the following year, 1564, the ducal accountants took in hand the audit of the accounts presented by Baldini at the end of his term of office and discovered that those accounts did not square. To explain what had happened, one could not do better than let their colorful report speak for itself:

> In 1564 the auditing of this account took place with several books that end on the last day of February 1562 [Florentine dating, equivalent of 1563], which makes thirty months.
>
> The accountants in the course of the auditing could never extract from Bernardo or from other ministers of the mint the truth about their way of proceeding in this administration, because what was written did not show it; on the contrary several contradictions appeared, and in particular it seemed as though there should have been minted more from a pound of silver than Bernardo gave account for. To be sure to understand the transactions, the said accountants moved to the mint, and while they watched the weighing and counting of two lots of silver coins of around 23 pounds each, they uncovered the fault in the scales and in the weights in relation to the correct weight at which Bernardo received the silver. All this occurred in the presence of the said Bernardo. . . . The difference depends on several counts, but the most important thing is his having minted out of every

23. ASF, Atti degli Ufficiali di Monte e Soprasindaci 21, ins. 27.

> pound of silver 73 lire and 12 soldi, whereas he put in the accounts not even 72 lire 14 soldi.[24]

In other words, the auditors discovered that the mint scales had been tampered with and that from a given amount of metal, more money was coined than was legally authorized and reported.

The auditing of the accounts started in 1564. The report from which the passage above is quoted is dated 2 July 1571. Evidently, for reasons I have not been able to identify, it took a long time for the affair to be clarified. However, after the inquiry the affairs of the mint improved immediately. From 1564 to 1570, the data on mintings show that the creeping debasement was completely halted (see app. 7, table A4, col. *c*). Francesco (for I suppose that it was he who pulled the strings) took advantage of the situation and appointed a commission of experts composed of Marcello Acciaiuoli, Gio. Battista de' Servi, Agnolo Biffoli, and Giovanni Dini. The commission was charged with "understanding and reporting on what had been done at the Ducal mint and by its Ministers"; "having considered past transgressions," furthermore, it should give advice on "the best way to coin gold and silver in the future."[25] The conclusions and recommendations of the experts were the following: (1) that the gold coin be struck, as in the past, at a fineness of 22 carats and at the rate of 100 1/2 scudi per pound, which resulted in a weight of 3.38 grams each;[26]

24. ASF, Atti degli Ufficiali di Monte e Soprasindaci 16. Explicit references to the "transgression" of the master of the mint both in the minting activity and in the exchange and withdrawal of forbidden foreign coins are found also in ASF, Zecca 115, c. 236.

25. ASF, Zecca, Fiorinaio, cc. 190v, 191r.

26. "If the mint master went up to 100 2/3 scudi per pound (weight) it should be tolerated, but no more than that."

(2) that whoever brought gold to the mint should be credited with 99 2/3 scudi for every pound of 22 carats as in the past;[27] (3) that the various silver coins be aligned and struck on the basis of 109 1/2 giulii for every pound of popolino silver, which meant coins for the amount of 73 lire per pound of popolino silver (which in turn meant a parity of 4.46 grams of pure silver for a lira);[28] (4) that whoever brought silver or foreign coins the mint would pay them currency "as for many years it has been customary," that is, on the basis of 71 lire 5 soldi 9 denari for every pound of silver of popolino fineness.[29] The experts' report is dated 30 June 1571. It was transformed into an ordinance with the ducal rescript and made executive the following 3 and 4 July.[30]

Since the previous coinages had been based on approximately 73 1/2 lire of silver coins per pound of popolino silver, the new ceiling of 73 lire per pound meant a revaluation of the currency in terms of silver on the order of 0.7 percent. The mint accounts are there to prove that the new parity was strictly observed and maintained. Francesco was not joking. The holy terror of incurring his wrath stands out in a letter sent to him by those in charge of the mint, dated 18 April 1575. In it they reported that after the order of 1571 to strike silver

27. The difference between the scudi 100 1/2 extracted from a pound of gold of 22 carats and the scudi 99 2/3 paid to merchants and money changers had to cover production costs and seigniorage.

28. Since the value of the giulio was 13 soldi 4 denari, 109 1/2 giulii were the equivalent of 73 lire.

29. The official price of 71 lire 5 soldi 9 denari per pound of popolino silver is found in the mint documents as early as 1560 (see ASF, Zecca 119, 250). As already indicated, the difference between the 73 lire in coins extracted from a pound of popolino silver and the 71 lire 5 soldi 9 denari paid to merchants and money changers served to cover production costs and seigniorage.

30. The text of the report is reproduced in app. 2.

coins on the basis of 73 lire per pound of popolino, Carlo Buonaiuti, mint weigher, "for fear" of going over the established ceiling, issued coins at 72 lire 14 soldi or 72 lire 15 soldi per pound to the obvious detriment of the mint (the mint accounts confirm that between 1571 and 1575 the issues were below the rate of 73 lire per pound of popolino; see table A4, col. *c*).[31] They asked, moreover, that a greater margin of tolerance be granted with respect to the weight (this was granted) and they took the opportunity of proposing that the grand duke abandon the revaluation decreed in 1571 and allow them to coin on the basis of 73 lire 10 soldi 7 2/3 denari, as had been done in the years immediately preceding the reform. They made this request because, according to them, 73 lire per pound of popolino silver was not a competitive price and favored the flow of silver to other mints "that pay merchants more for the pound of silver than Your Serene Highness's Mint does." The grand duke answered tersely that he did not accept the proposal and "does not want to raise the price."[32]

The monetary order and the silver parity decreed in

31. The text of the letter is interesting and worth reproducing here: "In 1571, when coins were minted at 73 lire 10 soldi 7 2/3 denari per pound, it was ordered that in future they should be minted at 73 lire, that is, 109 1/2 giulii. According to Carlo Bonaiuti, the mint weigher, the late Agnolo Biffoli, treasurer, and the late Gio. Battista de' Servi ordered him to not allow issues to go above 73 lire per pound—and he said, it being technically impossible for him to strike coins exactly at that standard, he had not the heart to do so. Consequently they gave him a range from 109 to 109 1/2 giulii so that he could operate within that half giulio margin. Checking what is being done now, we find that minting is on the base of 72 lire 14 soldi or at 72 lire 15 soldi, but it does not reach 73 [lire] because Carlo, for fear of going above the limit, is always that half giulio less" (ASF, Zecca 90, c. 39).

32. Ibid.

July 1571 were rigorously adhered to throughout the following decades. Again in 1587, a few months before his death during a monetary and banking crisis, when some experts advised a devaluation, Francesco refused adamantly "because the intention of the grand duke was firm in not wishing to change either the weight or the fineness of the coins."[33] The reform, referred to more and more frequently as "the reform of four deputies of 4 July 1571," continued to hold sway and after Francesco's death was confirmed, as we shall see, by his brother Ferdinando in 1597.

The same authoritarian efficiency Francesco showed in blocking the issue of biglione coins and stabilizing the metallic content of silver coins emerges in his efforts to foster more complete monetary sovereignty, in the sense of reducing the circulation of foreign coins within his state. Proclamations aimed at eliminating foreign coins from domestic circulation were issued in Tuscany in 1552, 1556, 1557, and 1564.[34] The very frequency with which these bans were repeated suggests that they were unheeded. Already in the forties and fifties, however, the abundant flow of forbidden coins into the mint seems to indicate that the pressure applied to eliminate foreign coins was quite effective.[35] Under Francesco, the "searchers" were given further powers. This hated species had the authority to enter the shops and taverns, even private houses, and to inspect any and every drawer or chest, searching for the forbidden coins.[36] If these were

33. Ricci, *Cronaca*, p. 502.

34. See Cantini, *Legislazione toscana*. See also ASF, Leggi e Bandi, app. 65. The foreign coins to be eliminated were either of silver or of biglione. Foreign gold coins were generally accepted, apart from worn or underweight ones.

35. ASF, Zecca 190, 191.

36. See, for example, ASF, Zecca 115, c. 57, for October 1588: "the list of certain people who did not want to show their money to the

found, they were confiscated and the unlucky owner was also fined. The confiscated coins were handed over to the mint to be melted down and made into good Florentine coins, and the proceeds of both the reminting and the fine were divided among the searchers themselves, the mint, and, naturally, the grand duke, who never let an opportunity pass to get some money out of his "very happy" subjects.

Francesco pursued an almost fanatical policy of monetary stability from the 1560s, which consisted in the elimination of foreign coins, the abolition of the biglione coins, and the intrinsic stability of silver coins. These were different aspects of the same policy and were tightly linked to one another. One of the results was the stability of the silver parity of the money of account (lira). In fact, the second half of the sixteenth century stands out in Florence as a period of exceptional stability of the money of account in terms of silver. This can be seen clearly from table 7, in which the data referring to the parity between 1550 and 1600 are expressed in figures of two decimal points to enable us to detect the slight decline that occurred in the fifteen-year period from 1550 to 1565.

In the second half of the sixteenth century, the stability of the Florentine lira in terms of silver is exceptional, not only in a historical perspective but also in relation to the contemporary movements of other currencies. In the second half of the century the lire of Venice, Milan, and Genoa underwent a 20–30 percent devaluation in terms of silver.[37] It was in comparison with the relative weakness of other currencies that the fame of grand ducal management of the Tuscan currency was established.

---

searchers and who drew out their weapons and beat the searchers." See also cc. 76 and 79.

37. Cipolla, *Avventure della lira*, app. III, table A2.

TABLE 7. Secular debasement of Florentine lira di piccioli, 1300–1600.

Year	Parity of the Florentine lira in gm of pure silver	Devaluation in the preceding fifty years (%)
1300	19.0	
1350	11.1	42
1400	9.6	14
1450	8.8	8
1500	6.6	25
1550	4.62	30
1600	4.46	3.5

SOURCE: For the period 1300–1500, Bernocchi, *Monete della Repubblica*. For the period 1500–1600, see tables 4 and 5.

Stability in terms of silver did not necessarily mean stability in terms of goods and services, or of gold. For the movements of prices and wages, we have the index calculated by Parenti (agricultural prices have the preponderant weight in this index and consequently it reflects to an excessive degree agricultural movements and fluctuations). Between 1552 and 1600, with base 100 the average of the years 1610–20, the index moved as follows:[38]

1552:	50	1585:	76
1558:	71	1590:	78
1565:	64	1600:	103
1575:	86		

38. Parenti, *Prime ricerche*, p. 144.

Between 1552 and 1600 there was clearly a basic upward trend in prices and wages that reflected the gradual devaluation of silver, due mainly to the arrival on a large scale of white metal from the American continent. The tendency for prices to rise appears however to have been punctuated by two phases of recession: one taking place between 1558 and 1565 and the other, which was longer and more severe, between 1575 and 1590. We shall have occasion to return to the deflationary phase of 1575–90 in the epilogue.[39] Here it will be sufficient to note that silver tended to depreciate for the whole of the second half of the sixteenth century, not only in terms of goods and services but also in terms of gold. This depreciation created problems in the monetary and payments system that will be dealt with in the following chapter.

39. The phases indicated in the text may be seen in ibid., p. 169, graph 10, which shows the percentage deviation of the index from the trend.

CHAPTER FOUR

Gold Coins

IN THE FIRST chapter we saw that during the sixteenth century the florin was replaced by the scudo as the only gold coin in circulation. The numismatic history of the scudo during the course of the century is summarized in table 8. In it we can see that from its first appearance in 1530 and for the whole of the sixteenth century the scudo was devalued only twice: first in 1533 and again in 1548. The purpose of both devaluations was to attract greater quantities of gold to the mint.[1] The devaluation of 1533 was around 3 percent; the second, in 1548, was a minor touch-up of 0.5 percent. In practice, after the 1533 devaluation, the traditional policy of keeping the gold

1. The debasement of the currency encouraged people to bring metal to the mint because for a given quantity of metal the mint paid more money in nominal value. The ordinance of 1548 is explicit: "According to the provision of 7 November 1533, 100 scudi were minted per pound [of gold] out of which 99 were given to the merchants. From experience it has been seen that the mint remains almost without work if the said order is maintained; therefore it was decided that in the future 100 1/2 scudi be minted per pound from which the merchant be given 99 2/3 per pound" (ASF, Zecca, Fiorinaio, c. 190, 2 August 1548). Mint accounts in ASF, Zecca 190, c. 152, dated September 1548, and ASF, Zecca 150, confirm that the order was carried out.

TABLE 8. The intrinsic characteristics of the Florentine gold scudo, 1530–97.

Date	Theoretical fineness (carats)	Taglio (no. of pieces from 1 lb. of alloy)	*Resa* (no. of pieces given to merchants for 1 lb. of alloy)	Theoretical weight (gm)	Theoretical pure gold content (gm)	Official quotation (lire and soldi di piccioli)
1530 (June)	22.5	99–99 1/2		3.412–3.429	3.199–3.215	7.0
1533 (November)	22	100	99	3.395	3.112	
1535 (March)	22	100	99	3.395	3.112	7.5
1548 (August)	22	100 1/2	99.66	3.378	3.097	
1556	22	100 1/2	99.66	3.378	3.097	7.12
1571	22	100 1/2	99.66	3.378	3.097	7.12
1597	22	100 1/2	99.66	3.378	3.097	

NOTE: The difference between the taglio and the yield represented the brassaggio (cost of minting) plus the seigniorage. The theoretical weight was calculated by dividing the weight of the pound by the taglio. The fine content has been calculated by multiplying the weight by the fineness. Both the fineness and the weight had an admitted tolerance (*rimedio*) which both in 1571 and 1597 was 0.16 percent for weight and "half an eighth of a carat per ounce."

coin stable in its metallic content was pursued once more. Caution was also used as regards silver coins and biglione, and from 1565 onward the silver currency remained absolutely stable and no more biglione were minted. However, between 1530 and 1565 there was, on the whole, a considerable differential in the debasement of silver and biglione coins, on the one hand, and gold, on the other. This fact, together with others to be discussed later, created pressure on the exchange rate of gold coins.

From the very first coining of the florin, the authorities continually came up against the progressive increase in the exchange value of gold coins in terms of the money of account, based on the silver and biglione coins. The exchange rate of the florin, which was 20 soldi piccioli (1 lira) in 1252, had reached 140 soldi (7 lire) by the end of the fifteenth century. Since the florin had remained practically the same in weight and fineness throughout the centuries of its existence, the increase in its exchange value could be ascribed to two circumstances: an increase in the exchange ratio between gold and silver in favor of gold, and the progressive debasement of silver money and biglione to which the money of account (lira-soldo) was tied. In reality, in the second half of the thirteenth century, the gold-to-silver ratio had been gradually increasing in favor of gold and by the beginning of the fourteenth century had reached, albeit temporarily, the level of 1:13 or even 1:14 (that is, 13 or 14 units of silver were needed to buy 1 unit of gold). From the middle of the fourteenth century, however, the gold-to-silver ratio tended to remain stable around the value of 1:10. The gradual increase from the second half of the fourteenth century onward in the exchange rate of gold coins was, therefore, almost exclusively caused by the deterioration of silver and biglione coins (see table 4). This fact reinforced the traditional conviction that any rise in the exchange rate of gold was the result of a perverse and improper management of money.

During the first three decades of the sixteenth century the exchange rate of gold coins (florins) on the Florentine market remained stable at 7 lire. The years 1530 and 1531, however, saw a period of successive debasements of both silver and biglione coins, as we have seen in chapter 3. These devaluations pushed up the exchange rate. When the Florentine gold scudo first appeared in June 1530, it was officially valued at 7 lire, which had been the value of the florin for the previous thirty years.[2] This exchange rate was confirmed in August 1531 when the florin (called ducato by that time) was quoted officially at 7 lire and 10 soldi.[3] In 1535 the scudo went to 7 lire 5 soldi, while the florin-ducato was aligned in parallel at 7 lire 15 soldi.[4] Some years later, perhaps around the time of the 1538 devaluation, the

2. The decree of 20 June 1530 that ordered the coining of the gold scudo contains no reference to the nominal value of the new coin (see Bernocchi, *Monete della Repubblica*, vol. 1, pp. 472–73). The decree of 4 August 1531 (p. 477), however, contains the following reference: "From the day in which the scudo was brought to 7 lire di piccioli in Florence, that is from 8 July 1530." The ordinance of 8 July 1530 followed only eighteen days after that of 20 June 1530: bearing in mind the time needed actually to start the process of minting, it can be safely argued that the Florentine gold scudo was officially valued at 7 lire from its first appearance.

3. Ibid., p. 476. The same information is also to be found in Varchi, *Storia fiorentina*, bk. 9, chap. 57. See also the manuscript *Diario* in ASF, Bardi, sez. 3, b. 14.

4. The text of ordinance of 5 March 1535 (ASF, Zecca, Fiorinaio, cc. 184v–185r, reproduced also by Cantini, *Legislazione toscana*, vol. 1, pp. 84–90) speaks of gold ducats valued at "one gold scudo and 10 soldi" and later of "gold scudi at 7 lire and 5 soldi each." The presentation is so confused that it is difficult to make head or tail of it. An unexpected source of assistance is the bookkeeper who compiled the "yellow book to keep the accounts of the taxes of the Comuni and other taxpayers" (ASF, Monte Comune, 2071 c. Ov). Under the date

TABLE 9. Official value of the florin-ducato and the scudo in lire and soldi di piccioli, 1529–42.

Date	Florin-ducato	Scudo
1529	7	
1530 (July)		7
1531 (August)	7.10	7
1535 (March)	7.15	7.5
1538		7.10
1542	8.7	7.10

official exchange rate of the gold scudo was further raised to 7 lire 10 soldi.[5] In 1542 when the last gold ducati were coined at a slightly lighter weight than the traditional florin they were officially given the value of 8 lire 7 soldi each. Table 9 schematizes movements between 1529 and 1542.

In the second half of the century the situation changed radically, despite a facade of apparent continuity (we must bear in mind that, as explained in the

1569, that clerk explains the intricacies in the following terms: "In the year 1534 [Florentine dating; 1535] it was ordered by law that every [gold] ducat be paid one gold scudo and 10 soldi; the value of the gold scudo was in the said time 7 lire and 5 soldi; adding the 10 soldi, the value of the said ducat came to 7 lire 15 soldi."

5. On the devaluation of 1538 see chap. 3, above. The official value of the gold scudo at 7 lire 10 soldi must already have been in force before 1541. In fact, in the *Giornale bianco* marked F in the Salviati archive (Scuola Normale Superiore, Pisa, Archivio Salviati, Libri di Commercio, serie I, no. 809) in c. 79 it can be seen that in August 1541 the company had received 2,060 gold scudi valued at 7 lire and 10 soldi per scudo. The company, however, paid out some of these scudi at a higher exchange rate and some at a lower rate. The

first chapter, at the end of the 1540s the florin-ducato disappeared from circulation and the scudo became the piece around which these events revolved). In 1556 it was observed that gold coins were "willingly extracted by the State."[6] At an exchange rate of 7 lire 10 soldi, the Tuscan gold scudo was evidently undervalued. In order to protect the Florentine scudo and keep it within the borders of the state, an ordinance was issued on 15 July and renewed the following January, in which it was established "that in future the Florentine scudo [should] be worth 7 lire 12 soldi and the other scudi of whatever mint and type should remain at the usual rate of 7 lire and 10 soldi."[7]

In order to justify the different treatments accorded to the Florentine scudi and foreign scudi, the ordinance stated that "the Florentine scudi coined in the city of Florence with the ducal stamp and insignia are of a better fineness and greater value than the other scudi as far as fineness and weight are concerned." The argument was specious. The fact was that a much more rigid policy was in the offing, one of decidedly intransigent resistance to further rises in the exchange rate of gold coins,

---

mint paid "good gold scudi" at the rate of 7 lire 10 soldi each in 1543 (ASF, Zecca 190, c. 20v).

In this period the mint made additional profits in a rather unorthodox way by withdrawing banned foreign scudi at 7 lire 6 soldi and reselling them at 7 lire 10 soldi to a certain Bruno, a banker, who undertook to export them. Thus, for example, on 9 June 1544 the mint registered a credit of "4 lire 16 soldi out of a profit from 24 banned scudi changed here at the mint for 7 lire 6 soldi each and given to Bruno the banker at 7 lire 10 soldi each to be sent abroad." For this and similar cases, see ASF, Zecca 190, cc. 55v, 71, 78, 95, 124.

6. Less than two years later it was noted also in Milan that "gold increases in price every day" (Archivio di Stato di Milano, Registri Panigarola 19, c. 214, 18 February 1558).

7. ASF, Zecca, Fiorinaio, c. 190 (15 July 1566). See also ASF, Leggi e Bandi, app. 65.

and this policy was applied more vigorously to the foreign scudi.

The rise in the exchange rate of gold coins between 1530 and 1544 was due, on the whole, to the same factors that had triggered the rise in the exchange rate of the florin from the middle of the thirteenth century, that is, the weakness of the silver and biglione coins. This fact reinforced the widespread conviction that every rise was the consequence and evidence of improper monetary manipulations. Not everybody was ready to recognize that the scenario was changing dramatically and that from the middle of the century the value of gold coins was propelled upward, not by the debasement of silver coins and biglione, but rather by the depreciation of silver with respect to gold following the arrival in Europe of large quantities of the former from the Americas. The school of thought with which Jean Bodin was to clash in France had its counterpart in Tuscany.

Francesco de' Medici was the least ready to understand the new situation. In his view the stability of the exchange rate of gold coins, the suspension of the coinage of biglione coins, and the stability of the metallic content of silver coins were to be considered as basically the same thing. The commission of experts he had nominated in the summer of 1571 to put some order into the monetary system, and to discourage the "past transgressions" that had taken place in the mint, strengthened him in his opinions. In their final report, they submitted the idea that "nothing causes the price of gold to rise like the debasement of money; moreover the worse it gets, the more Your Majesty's revenues decrease, and so do the liquid assets of the people."[8]

8. See the complete report in app. 2.

Every rise in the exchange value of gold coins was the evil fruit of speculation as far as Francesco was concerned. In his view this was doubly reprehensible—it disturbed that healthy equilibrium that he thought to have established once and for all; and it might have a negative effect on his revenues, as his experts had intimated, an idea that was intolerable to his grasping nature.[9] The result was a continuous confrontation between the geometric mentality and obstinate, imperious character of Francesco, who wanted to stabilize the exchange value of gold coins, on the one hand, and the irresistible forces of the market, which tended to raise their exchange rate, on the other.

As we have seen, in 1556 it had already been acknowledged that gold scudi (see fig. 6) were "willingly extracted by the State," and consequently the exchange rate of the scudo rose to 7 lire 12 soldi. This rise was limited to Florentine scudi alone; foreign scudi were to continue being exchanged at the rate of 7 lire 10 soldi. Insofar as the official exchange rate of 7 lire 10 soldi was really adhered to, the foreign scudi were undervalued and therefore tended to leave the Florentine state. In 1563 the monetary authorities were forced to admit that there was "a scarcity and lack of gold scudi in this market [Florence] as well as in all the other markets in Italy." Bankers and money changers had to be authorized to pay bills of exchange, which were traditionally denominated in gold, with silver coins, a practice that allowed them to include in the exchange a premium (agio) in

9. From the registers of the Monte Comune it appears, however, that the taxes due to that administration were revalued in relation to the increase in the market exchange rate. See, for example, ASF, Monte Comune 2071.

FIG. 6. The gold scudo of Francesco de' Medici.
O. FRA · MED · MAG · DVX · AETRIAE · II
R. OBIS · DEI · VIRTU · SESTN ·
O∅2.5 3.4g

favor of gold coins.[10] Six years later, in 1569, the market rate for the scudo had risen to 7 lire 14 soldi, while the official rate stayed at 7 lire 10 soldi for foreign scudi and 7 lire 12 soldi for Florentine scudi.[11] The official rate presupposed a gold-to-silver ratio of 1:10.7 and 1:10.9,

10. See chap. 1, n. 43. In 1562–63 we learn from the accounts of the Pisa arsenal "that the workforce intends to be, and has been, paid in gold scudi at the exchange rate of 7 lire and 10 soldi per scudo" (Angiolini, "Arsenale," p. 71). The workforce demanded payment in gold scudi at the official rate of exchange, which undervalued the scudi because they could later sell the scudi on the market at a higher quotation. In the accounts of the treasury of 1565, the scudi are entered at the exchange rate of 7 lire and 10 soldi but higher rates also appear. The difference, known as the agio (premium) varied from 0.5 to 1 percent. See ASF, Depositeria generale, 772 c. 40 (6 October 1565); c. 32 (28 April 1565); c. 35 (30 June 1565); cc. 36–37 (11 August 1565).

11. The passage by the Monte Comune bookkeeper mentioned in n. 4, above, states that "today 1569 the gold scudo is worth 7 lire 14 soldi."

whereas the market ratio was 1:11.[12] The consequences of this situation were what one would expect: not only was gold slow in flowing to the mint, but the gold coins in circulation tended to emigrate elsewhere. Whoever wanted gold scudi had to pay more than the official price for them, and since Francesco's bans seem to have been an effective deterrent, those who dealt in scudi used to ask for a premium on top of the official rate rather than bargain for a higher exchange rate, which boiled down to the same thing.

During 1573 the situation deteriorated considerably. The exchange ratio between gold and silver on the market had risen to 1:11.5 and 1:11.7, and consequently the market rate for the scudo (official rate plus premium) had risen to 8 lire and more.[13] The chronicler Giuliano de' Ricci, taking the side of the grand duke, wrote that "on account of the merchants' greed" the situation had precipitated into "an uproar . . . a confusion, and an enormous mess."[14] Francesco was, in fact, obstinate and stubborn and did not desist. In November of the same year he issued a new decree, which, with complete disregard for market forces, peremptorily ordered that "in

12. In 1569 a scudo contained 3.097 grams of pure gold (see table 8). Since in 1569 an average of 73 1/2 lire of silver coins were minted per pound of popolino silver (see app. table 4), the silver parity of the lira came to 4.427 grams of pure silver. At an exchange rate of 7 lire 10 soldi, the 3.097 grams of pure gold of the scudo were thus the equivalent of 33.20 grams of pure silver (gr 4,427 × 7.5). This gave a ratio of gold to silver 1:10.7. The exchange rate of 7 lire 12 soldi meant a ratio of 1:10.9. A market rate of 7 lire 14 soldi meant a ratio of 1:11.

13. In the report of 1573, which will be discussed later in this book, two of the experts maintained that the scudo was worth 8 lire or even 8 lire 3 soldi on the market (see app. 4). These rates of exchange implied ratios of gold to silver of 1:11.5 and 1:11.7, respectively.

14. Ricci, *Cronaca*, p. 67.

no way, in a bank or elsewhere, should a higher price be paid" than 7 lire 10 soldi for the foreign scudo and 7 lire 12 soldi for the Florentine scudo, and that the exchange rate "be still."[15]

"Be still" could by this time be used as the motto of grand ducal monetary policy, which by trying to impose order managed to be the source of disorder. The confusion created by the grand duke's monetary policy consisted not only in the growing divergence between the official rate and the market rate, but also in the fact that there were several market rates, whose wide range reflected the great variety of bargaining powers and different degrees of propensity, on the part of dealers, to risk infringing the law. It was an "uproar," as Ricci called it, in which the wide variety of premiums requested on the market served only to accentuate uncertainty.

The problem became acute for bills of exchange, which had traditionally been paid in gold coins. In 1573, Francesco, who was increasingly irritated by the uproar, appointed a commission of experts to study the problem. The commission consisted of Carlo Pitti, Napoleone Cambi, Benedetto Busini, and Giovan Battista de' Servi, who were charged with sounding out the opinion of a wider circle of experts and bringing back the results of the inquiry to the court. The four commissioners called the "majority of merchants who negotiate in the market and transact daily in exchanges," that is, twenty-two of the most influential names in the contemporary Florentine financial world.

The experts did not agree either in their analysis of the basic causes of the uproar or in possible solutions.

15. ASF, Leggi e Bandi, app. 65 (November 1573). Cantini, *Legislazione toscana*, vol. 8, p. 75, reproduces the decree, but because of a misprint the grand ducal gold scudo appears erroneously valued in this text at 7 lire 10 soldi.

Some maintained that for at least a year and a half the payment of bills of exchange in gold coins at the official rate should be imposed by law. Others proposed that the choice of paying in gold or silver coins (from the giulio upward) be left open, and that if the debtor were willing to pay in gold, the scudo be valued at a more realistic rate than the official one. Those who sustained this last thesis disagreed among themselves both about the means of recognizing the lesser value of silver and about the size of the difference. Some argued that the official rate should remain the same, but that a premium on gold of about 3 or 3 1/2 percent be made legal, while others favored the official recognition of a rise in the exchange rate. Among those in favor of the last solution, some proposed an official exchange rate of the scudo of 7 lire 14 soldi, and others proposed a differentiated exchange rate of 7 lire 16 soldi for the Florentine scudi and 7 lire and 14 soldi for non-Florentine scudi.

Once these discordant opinions had been gathered, the four members of the commission disagreed over how to present the results of their inquiry. They divided themselves into two groups: Carlo Pitti and Giovan Battista de' Servi on the one hand and Benedetto Busini and Napoleone Cambi on the other.

The general level of the discussion was not very subtle; on the contrary it was both confused and oversimplified. One must, however, recognize that the situation was extremely complicated. Not only was there a gold crisis, but the banks operating on the Florentine market were going through a severe liquidity crisis: it seemed as though silver coins had also disappeared, and whoever wished to take them out of the banks had to pay a premium (agio). This situation helped to confuse the experts' ideas further, since many of them could not distinguish between the consequences of the rise in the gold-to-silver ratio and the consequences of the liquidity crisis in the banking system. As far as gold was concerned, however, at least Benedetto Busini and Napoleone Cambi seem to have grasped the real issue in their final report.

It was unthinkable, they maintained, to keep scudi on the Florentine market at an exchange rate of 7 lire 10 soldi or even 7 lire and 12 soldi. Elsewhere gold had a higher value; being thus undervalued, gold tended to emigrate from Tuscany.

> Those who have scudi send them where they are worth more . . . than the 7 lire 10 soldi or 7 lire 12 soldi at which they are valued here [in Tuscany], and particularly to Spain, from which all the [silver] species come and [where] the gold scudi is worth the equivalent of more than 8 lire 3 soldi per scudo. They [gold scudi] are also sent to Genoa, where almost all, or the greater part, of the coins that arrive in Italy end up, and where a gold scudo is worth 8 lire of Your Ducal money or more.[16]

In other words, according to Busini and Cambi, (1) the rise in the value of gold was due to the devaluation of silver; (2) the devaluation of silver coins was the consequence of the arrival of large quantities of silver on the market; (3) silver arrived in Italy from Spain; (4) it arrived principally via Genoa; (5) the undervaluation of gold at the official exchange rate favored the export of gold from Tuscany; and (6) gold coins were exported to Spain, where the scudo was exchanged for the equivalent of 8 lire 3 soldi in Florentine coins, and secondly to

16. For the unabridged text of the report see app. 4. The original answers of the experts whose opinion had been sought are to be found in ASF, Zecca 115.

Genoa, where the scudo was exchanged for the equivalent of 8 lire in Florentine coins.[17]

Although they started from these observations, which were full of realism and common sense, they arrived paradoxically at totally contradictory conclusions: that is, that it would have been "pernicious" to raise the official value of the scudo, because "if it ever happened, as it could, that there arrived on the market less silver and more gold, prices would return to their correct level, that is, about 7 lire 12 soldi per scudo." It is impossible to say if this tightrope-walking logic was sincere or dictated by the courtier's desire not to contradict Francesco's well-known opinions. In the rescript of 7 January 1574, however, Francesco's comment on the long memorandum was terse and hurried: "The argument on gold does not please His Highness in the least nor does the increase in the premium of 3 and 3 1/2 percent."[18]

This disagreement between the experts clearly favored Francesco's obstinacy. Thus a vicious circle was set in motion: the more the market pushed the more Francesco refused to budge, and the more he refused to budge the more his decrees increased tension on the market. A few months after the rescript of 7 January 1574, in August of the same year, Francesco abrogated the 1563 decree that had made it legal to put a premium on gold coins in the assessment of the value of the scudo, whenever bills of exchange were paid in silver

17. Ibid. In fact the Spanish authorities had raised the official exchange rate between gold and silver to 1:12.12 in 1566 not only to prevent gold from leaving the country but also to attract it there (Hamilton, *American Treasure*, pp. 61, 71). At the same time the official bimetallic ratio in Florence was 1:10.7 and 1:10.9 and the market rate was 1:11 (see nn. 12 and 13 above).

18. See below in app. 4 the grand ducal postscript to the report of 1573.

coins. The new decree declared all premiums illegal and once more established strict adherence to the exchange rate of 7 lire 10 soldi, which by now had become an obsession for Francesco.[19] In August 1577 Francesco wheeled out the argument once more and reiterated: "It is not permissible to pay or receive any scudo at a higher value than 7 lire and 10 soldi."[20]

Francesco was extraordinarily hard-headed. The Venetian ambassador Alvise Buonrizzo wrote of him: "His Highness is rather, not to say very, obstinate in his opinions and, when he has fixed on one decision there is no human means of making him change it." This stubbornness was aggravated by the fact that although he could ask the opinions of others he would not accept their advice. "His Highness does not want anyone to advise him in either State affairs or any other matter."[21]

It must be recognized that Francesco had no evil intentions; he wanted only a stable, balanced, and well-ordered market. However, as the old proverb says, the streets of hell are paved with good intentions. Gold coins, which were undervalued in Tuscany, went elsewhere, and the Florentine market found gold coins drained from circulation. On the first of July 1580, Baltazar Suarez wrote to Simon Ruíz from Florence that "*aquí no se alla un escudo.*"[22] On 10 August 1583 the Carnesecchi and Strozzi company stipulated a loan (*asiento*) to Philip II. The powerful Florentine company undertook to pay out 300,000 gold scudi to the Spanish king. Since it could not find gold coins on the market it paid the

19. Cantini, *Legislazione toscana*, vol. 8, p. 153 (30 August 1574). See also ASF, Leggi e Bandi, app. 65.

20. ASF, Leggi e Bandi, app. 65 (12 August 1577).

21. Segarizzi, *Relazioni*, vol. 3, part 2, pp. 17–18.

22. Ruíz Martin, *Lettres marchandes*, p. 50.

agreed amount in silver giulii.[23] Less than two years later, in June 1585, Grand Duke Francesco himself was obliged to write to the Spanish ambassador Don Pedro de Mendoza, who had asked for a loan in gold: "At the moment very few gold scudi are to be found here [in Florence] and they are very expensive . . . and there seems to be such a scarcity that it would be difficult to get together 10,000 in a short time, and even if there were a month I do not think that one could have 25,000, which is not a considerable sum."[24]

It must have cost him a great deal psychologically to have to make such an admission.

23. Ibid., p. LXI.
24. Ibid., p. LXII.

CHAPTER FIVE

Mint Issues

WE MUST now consider the levels and the trends of both the volume and value of issues of the Florentine mint. The mint had, from its origins, worked on commission, that is, it minted coins for citizens who brought it gold or silver in the form of rods, ingots, or foreign coins.

The weight, fineness, and design of the various coins the mint produced were severely regulated by law and the authorities, but the volume of the mintings and their breakdown into the various species of coin was left to the discretion of market forces. During the sixteenth century, the dukes and grand dukes occasionally had coins minted for themselves, but in these cases they behaved like any other private citizens.

Transactions were carried out as follows. An individual, who could be a foreigner, took metal to the mint or had it taken by a trustworthy representative. The mint credited him with an amount based on an officially established price. Within a few days or weeks, depending on how much work there was, the mint delivered coins for the amount credited to the individual in person or to his representatives. Both the name of the person for whom the transaction was undertaken and that of his representative were usually entered in the mint registers.[1] The dealer who took or had the metal taken to the mint could request that the corresponding amount in coins be credited to a third party to whom the mint would deliver the coins. This sort of triangular transaction was used often in the payment of taxes, when private dealers, money changers, bankers, or merchants took in receipts in foreign coins and were indebted to the ducal treasury for taxes or duty payable in Florentine coins.

In the periods of high minting activity there was a great deal of coming and going of individuals laden with precious metals and coins between the mint and the houses and shops of merchants, bankers, and money changers.

The mint acted as a monopoly as regards issues and a monopsony as regards the withdrawal of foreign coins. It was run for profit, two-thirds or three-quarters of which went to the duke as master of the mint, with the remaining going to the manager.[2] Normally the mint covered its running costs and made a profit by crediting those who brought metal to the mint with a sum inferior to what the mint itself made from the metal it received. Thus, for example, between 1533 and 1547, the mint credited anyone who brought a pound of gold with 99 scudi while it coined 100 scudi from this same amount of gold (see table 8). Other examples relate to silver coins. The provision of 5 March 1535 prescribed, for the coining of the giulio, that the mint extract 101 1/4 pieces from every pound of popolino silver and that the merchants

1. Each delivery of coins to a citizen or his messenger was called *sorte* (from the verb *sortire*, i.e., "come out"). The number of coins in a *sorte* were entered up as *mane* of four units each: thus, for example, "two and a half *mane* of piastre" meant "10 piastre" ([4 × 2] + 4/2 = 10).

2. ASF, Sindaci 19 (28 February 1587), 21, ins. 27 (18 August 1590).

be given 99 of these (see table 2). The July 1571 reform laid down that the mint should coin silver pieces of whatever type to a value of 73 lire from a pound of popolino silver, and that the merchants should receive the equivalent of 71 lire 5 soldi and 9 denari.[3] Up to this point everything looks simple and straightforward and can be usefully summarized in the formula P + (C + S) = M, where P stands for the official price paid by the mint for the precious metal (gold or silver), C stands for its cost of production, S for seigniorage, and M for the amount of coins produced by the mint out of the precious metals received.

In practice, however, things were neither simple nor straightforward. The mint in theory had no room for maneuver on the parameter of the number of coins to be extracted from a given quantity of metal, even if, as we have already seen, between 1550 and 1565 instances of abuse were not unknown. At the same time, the mint had wide margins of play with returns, for the following reason: the monetary authorities usually indicated the official price on the basis of which the mint manager was to pay for the metal brought to the mint (P in the formula above), but when metal in the form of foreign or prohibited coins was involved, the mint did not consider itself bound by the official price and, as contemporary documents say, "it bargained." Thus, for example, in 1543 and 1544 the official price that the mint should have paid for a pound of popolino silver was 68 lire 15 soldi 6 denari. Instead the mint, exploiting its monopsonistic position, withdrew prohibited coins, paying only 67 lire 19 soldi 9 denari per pound for them.[4] In

3. See app. 2.

4. ASF, Zecca 190, cc. 17v, 20v, 56. For the official price of 68 lire 15 soldi 6 denari the pound of popolino silver see ASF, Zecca 150.

1562 the official price that the mint should have paid for silver was 71 lire 5 soldi and 9 denari per pound of popolino (958.333/1000).[5] The Spanish reals with a fineness of 11 ounces 4 denari (930.556/1000) should consequently have been paid at 69 lire 4 soldi 5 denari the pound. On 9 and 25 May the mint, on the contrary, paid Niccolò and Francesco Capponi 68 lire 10 soldi 3 denari per pound for them.[6] Between 1576 and 1579 the mint almost always paid reals at 11 ounces 4 denari fineness on the basis of 69 lire the pound.[7] An account dated 22 October 1576 bears the following note: "Reals at 69 lire 5 soldi the pound, those which are of good fineness; the others should either be returned or new agreements be made; the 6 November agreement was reached with

5. ASF, Zecca 119.

6. ASF, Zecca 192, c. 19.

7. ASF, Zecca 137. The Spanish reals and other foreign coins were accepted by the mint on the basis of an estimate of their fineness according to the type of coin (reals of Toledo, reals of Seville, old reals, new reals). In ASF, Zecca 124, c. 2 (1 February 1574), the account made out to "Antonio Salazar and Lesme da Stodiglia [*sic*] Spanish merchants" contains the following credits: 1,055 1/2 pounds of reals of Toledo, fineness 11.1 ounces at 68 lire 5 soldi the pound; 403 1/2 pounds of reals of Seville, fineness 11.3 ounces at 68 lire 13 soldi the pound; 151 pounds of old reals with fineness of 11.5 ounces, 69 lire 5 soldi the pound.

It sometimes happened that when the coins were assayed they would show a lower fineness than had originally been assumed. In these cases, the mint either paid a lower price or returned the consignment and canceled the transaction. Thus, for example, on 30 August 1575, "a deduction was made from the 725 pounds of reals brought by Luigi and Alessandro Capponi because their fineness, instead of being 11 ounces 5 denari, in reality was at 11 ounces 2 denari; thus the price paid was reduced accordingly in agreement with Raffaello da Empoli, their cashier" (ASF, Zecca 215, c. 61). On the same day, "a reduction of the price paid was made in agreement with the above mentioned Raffaello on 195 pounds of reals received

Francesco Giorgini that up to four-fifths be paid [at] 69 lire 5 soldi and one-fifth [at] 68 lire 15 soldi."[8]

In the 1540s, especially before the great wave of silver arrived from Spain and Genoa and when gold still flowed into the mint in substantial quantities, the Florentine mint made profits in even less orthodox ways. Thanks to its double role as monopolist and monopsonist, the mint bought prohibited foreign gold coins that people were forced to relinquish at reduced prices, and instead of having them melted down and reminted sold the same coins to bankers and merchants at higher prices, on the condition that the merchants and bankers undertake to spend them outside the state.[9]

---

from them [the Capponi] that were of a lesser fineness than the usual ones."

Consignments were returned in the following instances: on 20 September 1574, "to the Ricci bank, credit canceled for 15 pounds of reals returned to the bank because they were of inferior fineness" (ASF, zecca 214, c. 7); on 29 March 1574, "557 pounds of reals at 69 lire 5 soldi the pound of 11 ounces 5 denari returned because of their inferior fineness" (ASF, Zecca 215, c. 30).

8. ASF, Zecca 137, account made out to Raffaello Torrigiani.

9. Besides that quoted in chap. 4, n. 5, the following cases are worth mentioning: 2 November 1544, "2 lire 16 soldi, which are the profits made on 14 banned scudi changed here in the mint at 7 lire 6 soldi each from the first of October up to today and then given to Bruno the banker for 7 lire 10 soldi to be sent abroad"; and another dated 20 January 1545, "2 lire of profit made on 10 scudi changed as above and given to Federigo de' Ricci to be sent abroad, that is, through the bank" (ASF, Zecca 190, c. 71). The gold coins that were relinquished with the undertaking that they be exported were often *sugellati*, that is, sealed in bags.

Similar transactions were made with banned silver coins; the latter were however never put back into circulation, even outside the state, but cut and sold as metal. For example, on 9 October 1544 there is record of "a profit made out of 17 pounds of silver in Roman coins that have been changed here in the mint at the rate of 64 lire 4

The mint's method of operating was not only unorthodox—it bordered on the illicit. The grand dukes willingly turned a blind eye because they partook fully in the division of the cake; and when there were cakes to be divided neither Cosimo nor his son Francesco held back. The practice was, however, not aboveboard and at a certain point a very influential person at court intervened. Carlo Antonio Dal Pozzo was judge of the *Tribunale della Ruota* in Florence in 1572 and *Auditore Fiscale* in 1574, and in 1582 he was named archbishop of Pisa, on which he left his *Fiscale* post but was kept on in the *Magnifico Consiglio* and in the *Pratica Segreta*. At one point he stepped in to bring a degree of integrity to the mint's activities. We do not know the exact date of this intervention, but from the bare indications in our possession it seems that it took place in the months immediately following the death of the grand duke Francesco. In the report of the mint auditors, dated August 1590, one can in fact read that whereas for the period from 1 September 1585 to 28 February 1588 the mint manager declared a profit of 4,377 florins (of account) "resulting from prohibited coins, confiscated coins, and those voluntarily delivered, . . . from the said time he [the manager] has credited nothing because of the order of the archbishop of Pisa to pay for the said coins their correct value, and he [the manager] declares to have done this and for this reason there are no profits."[10]

Let us return to the mint's output. Two periods must be distinguished in trying to establish the level and trend of coinages. For the period extending from the beginning of the century to 1533 only one source is known, the

---

soldi 6 denari the pound and sold cut to Antonio Chozegli at 65 lire 5 soldi the pound" (ASF, Zecca 190, c. 71).

10. ASF, Sindaci 21, ins. 27 (18 August 1590).

mint record known as the Fiorinaio, which carries data on the weight of the metal coined only for a few widely distanced semesters without reference to the value of the coins minted. The data in question were published by Bernocchi in his work on the coins of the Florentine Republic.[11] From 1543 to 1589, on the contrary, numerous accounting registers of the mint are available. The degree of diligence with which these registers were kept varies over time: several contradictions are apparent and many problems of interpretation remain unsolved. However, by putting together and comparing the pieces of the jigsaw puzzle, with infinite patience, a reasonably continuous series of data for the years 1543–89 can be constructed.

Both the data from the first period, derived from the Fiorinaio, and those from the second period, from the mint accounts, refer to semesters running from 1 March to 31 August and from 1 September to the end of February. In common with all data regarding mint output in all countries in medieval and early modern eras, those from Florence for the sixteenth century also present marked variations between one semester and another and one year and another. Consequently, if the data available are sporadic and not continuous, great caution is needed in dealing with them. However, what emerges from the scarce and scattered data for the period 1500–1533 ties in very well with the wider and continuous documentation available for the later period.

In the five semesters from 1 March 1503 to 31 August 1505, an annual average of 958 kilograms of pure silver was minted into the corresponding amount of silver

11. Bernocchi, *Monete della Repubblica*, vol. 1, pp. 418, summary tables in vol. 3, pp. 70–71, 256–58. One must be careful in using the tables because they contain printing mistakes.

coins. In the same semesters an annual average of 41 kilograms of pure gold was minted into gold coins. Assuming an exchange rate of gold to silver of about 1:10 we can estimate that the value of the gold issues was the equivalent of around 410 kilograms of pure silver: much less than half the value of the silver issues. The fact that there was a substantial preponderance of silver minting is confirmed by the data for the three semesters from 1 September 1510 to the end of February 1512: the value of gold issues remained at less than half the corresponding value of silver issues.

In the period between June 1524 and August 1525 the situation seems to be reversed. As has been said, it would be dangerous to rely on data for only two isolated semesters, but the data for the six semesters from 1 September 1529 to 31 August 1532 confirm the new development. Between 1529 and 1532 gold coinages for an annual average of 136 kilograms of pure gold far outweighed in value the annual average minting of 648 kilograms of pure silver, since at a ratio of gold to silver of 1 to 10, gold coinages would be the equivalent of 1,360 kilograms of pure silver (see table 10).

When the series of data for the 1540s derived from the mint accounts begins, the situation that emerges from these registers ties in well with the situation sketched by the scanty data from the Fiorinaio for the period 1529–1532 (see table 11). If at the beginning of the 1530s the average yearly coinage of silver was around 648 kilograms of pure silver, by the 1540s it was 572 kilograms. For gold coinages, there was an annual average of 136 kilograms at the beginning of the 1530s against 113 kilograms in the 1540s. As can be seen, the figures square, at least in order of magnitude, and in any case agree in indicating a net preponderance in the value of gold emissions over silver.

TABLE 10. Volume of gold and silver coinages in the Florentine mint, 1503–32 (annual averages).

Period	No. of semesters considered	Gold 24 carats (kg)	Silver 1000/1000 (kg)
1503 (3/1)–1505 (8/31)	5	41	958
1510 (9/1)–1512 (2/28)	3	62	1,399
1524 (6/1)–1525 (8/31)	2 1/2	258	204
1529 (9/1)–1532 (8/31)	6	136	648

NOTE: See appendix 6 for the details of how the figures in this table were calculated. The figures for silver deal exclusively with the minting of silver coins and do not take biglione coinages into consideration.

TABLE 11. Volume of gold and silver coinages in the Florentine mint, 1543–89 (annual averages).

Period	Gold 24 carats (kg)	Silver 1000/1000 (kg)
1543–49	113	572
1550–57	70	260
1558–59	50	2.679
1560–69	36	2.902
1570–79	21	5.152
1580–89	19	5.584

NOTE: See appendix 8 for the details of how the figures in this table were calculated. The figures for silver deal exclusively with silver mintings and do not take biglione coinages into consideration.

The 136 kilograms of gold of the 1530s and the 113 kilograms of the following decade represent substantial quantities. If we accept Hamilton's calculations, in those two decades the gold imported into Seville was greater in value than imports of silver:[12] as for volume, the gold imports were around 1,445 kilograms a year in the 1530s and 2,496 kilograms in the 1540s. The gold coined in Florence in those two decades represented therefore about 11 and 5 percent, respectively, of the gold arriving in Spain from the Americas.[13]

Was there any connection between these two flows? Where did the gold that was coined in Florence come from in a turbulent period of wars and political turmoil? Why, from the mid 1520s almost to the end of the 1550s, was the value of gold coinage greater than that of silver? The answers are unknown. We have seen that the gold scudo tended to replace the florin (ducato), and it is possible that a large part of the gold coinages after 1533 represented the reminting of one coin into another. But the preponderance of gold coinages seems to have begun before 1533, and for the period from 1 March 1529 to the end of August 1532 the Fiorinaio data explicitly indicate that the high gold coinages of those semesters were almost exclusively coinages of ducati and not scudi.

Several clues may help to solve this puzzle, and they all point in the direction of France. The period was characterized by the substitution for the ducato of the scudo, of French origin. This substitution—as we have seen in chapter 1—occurred in Florence only in 1533,

12. Hamilton, *American Treasure*, p. 42.

13. As far as the 1530s are concerned, the percentage quoted rests on the hypothesis that the values calculated for Florentine coinage in the first years of the decade are valid for the whole of the decade.

later than in Genoa, Milan, and Venice, where it took place in 1508, 1520, and 1528, respectively. In Genoa and Milan the first coinage of the scudo occurred during periods of prolonged French military and political occupation. Florence was not occupied by the French but was invaded by French écu. The account books of Florentine merchant companies and banks for these years are full of references to French écu au soleil.

Following these clues we arrive in France, where, as F. Spooner has shown, in the first half of the sixteenth century the mints of the kingdom coined much gold and very little silver. The following hypothesis can thus be proposed: on account of a favorable trade balance and a differential in the gold-to-silver ratio (gold losing ground in the Iberian peninsula owing to the quantities arriving from the Indies), there must have been a massive influx of American gold to France. From France some of this gold may have flowed into Italy through French military expenditures as well as through trade and financial transactions.

In Florence, as we have seen, gold asserted its supremacy around 1525; this situation lasted into the second half of the century but was suddenly reversed in the course of 1558 (see graphs 1 and 2).

As rarely happens in history, there was no gradual change. There was on the contrary a radical discontinuity datable with absolute precision. In 1558 the silver coinage curve takes a sharp upward turn. The phase that follows shows silver coinages increasing progressively up to the exceptional level of over 5.2 tons of pure silver a year in the decade 1570–79 and 5.6 tons a year in the following decade (see table 11). In the meantime gold coinages declined drastically from 113 kilograms of pure gold a year in the 1540s to 70 kilograms in the 1550s, 36 kilograms in the 1560s, 21 kilograms in the

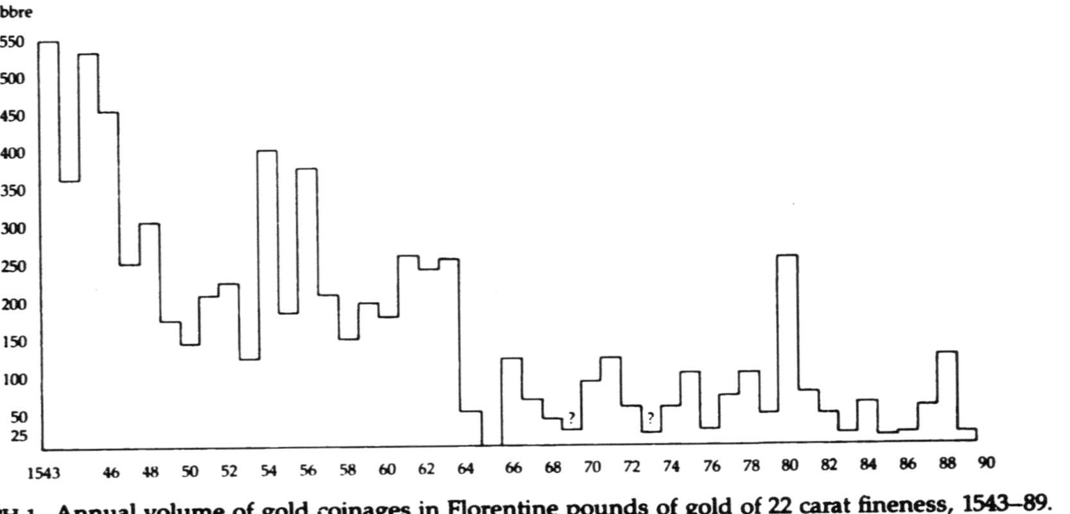

GRAPH 1. Annual volume of gold coinages in Florentine pounds of gold of 22 carat fineness, 1543–89. The data on which the graph has been constructed are in appendix 7, table A3 (the data in the appendix are half yearly, while those in the graph are yearly). The question mark indicates that the documentary evidence on coinages is either incomplete or missing.

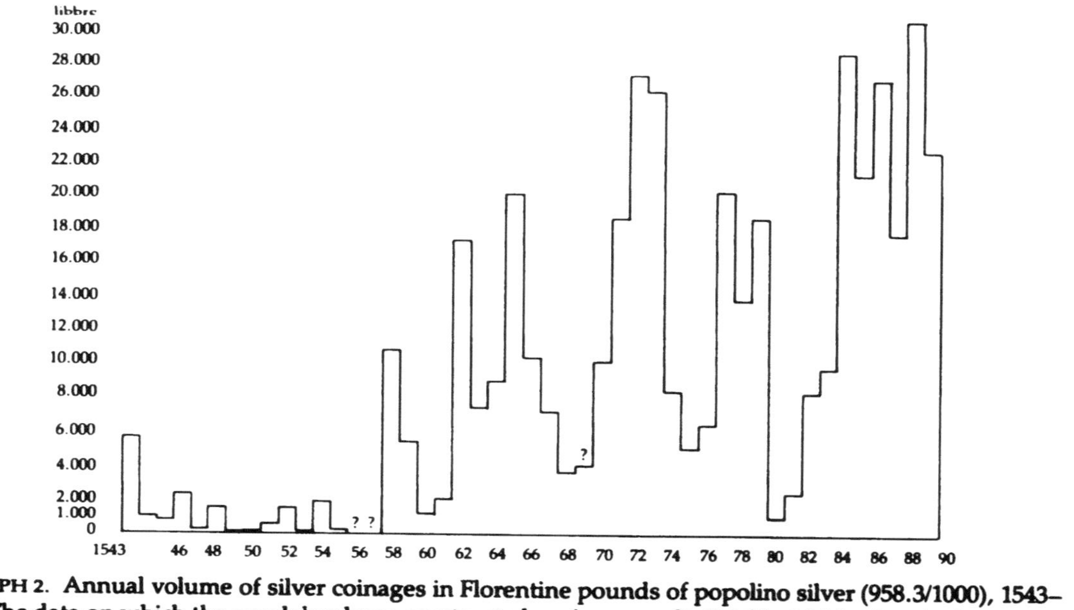

GRAPH 2. Annual volume of silver coinages in Florentine pounds of popolino silver (958.3/1000), 1543–89. The data on which the graph has been constructed are in appendix 7, table A4 (the data in the appendix are half yearly, while in the graph are yearly). The question mark indicates that the documentary evidence on the levels of coinages is either incomplete or missing.

1570s, and 19 kilograms in the 1580s (see table 11). This picture fits with what we have seen in the preceding chapter: since gold was undervalued in Florence, the Florentine monetary system was moving toward silver monometallism.

From the numismatic point of view the mint records show that between 1 September 1576 and 28 February 1590, out of a total of almost 17 million lire of silver coins minted, the composition of individual species was as follows:

Piastre	92 %
Testoni	5 %
Lire	0.2%
Giulii	1 %
Mezzi giulii	1.8%

The extraordinary influx of silver from 1558 caused a crisis in the mint and its organization. Coins were still produced by hand using the sole technology of the hammer. This technique revealed itself as inadequate to cope with the wave of silver that hit the mint from 1558. The old structures did not resist the impact. Long delays in consignments became increasingly frequent. For a lot of 43 kilograms of reals brought to the mint at the beginning of December 1560, the mint rendered the equivalent in Florentine coins in part on 18 January 1561 and the rest at the beginning of February:[14] these delivery times were obviously too long. To cope with the new situation it was decided to mechanize the production process using hydraulic power.[15] The technology had been developed in Germany; therefore German technicians were called in to erect the mill of the new mint on

14. Cipolla, *Argento spagnolo*, p. 485.
15. See Tucci, *Meccanizzazione*.

the banks of the Arno.[16] The new plant started operating in May 1576.[17] The new mint did not completely replace the old one, however. Gold and biglione coins continued to be coined in the old mint by traditional methods. As for silver, during the new plant's breaking-in period,

16. ASF, Zecca 136. Among the accounts relating to the setting up of new mint, on 1 August 1576 we find "9 lire spent to give the Germans to drink the three times that they minted since the foreman said that if they were not supplied with drink they wouldn't work well." On 31 December, once more: "2 lire spent for two flasks of white wine and fifteen pieces of bread and cheese so that the Germans would work."

17. The mechanization of coin production in the mint had already been considered by the autumn of 1565. In fact a gift of 50 florins for master Rosalino da Locarno, who had shown the duke "a way of minting coins with waterpower," is recorded in ASF, Depositeria generale, Registro 772, c. 40 (5 October 1565). However, for another ten years nothing more was done about it. In the eighteenth century, an antiquarian identified as Baldovinetti by L. Tondo (*Moneta nella Storia d'Europa*, p. 318) wrote that "in September of the year 1574 coins began to be minted by the use of waterpower in the German fashion, and they came out cleaner and shinier. The invention was German, and thus the grand duke Francesco I had a place built purposely outside the walls on the Arno toward the porta alla Croce." The information, however, is incorrect. The mint register ASF, Zecca 154 shows unequivocably that production at the new water-powered mint started not in September 1574 but on 16 May 1576.

In September 1576 the mint manager, Jacopo Pintelli, brought 16 testoni to court so that the grand duke could see for himself the quality of coins produced with the new techniques. The event is mentioned in the mint registers in the following terms: "[Paid] to his most serene Francesco Medici Grand Duke of Tuscany in the month of September 1576, 4 florins 4 lire in the form of sixteen new testoons made in the new mint and after having been told by messer Carlo Pitti, I, Jacopo Pintelli, took them to his Serene Highness's antechamber and gave them to signor Pandolfo Bardi, the Duke's master of the Chamber, who said he would take them to the Grand Duke and messer Carlo Pitti was present at this" (ASF, Zecca 137, c. 14). Pintelli was clearly proud of being admitted to court, even if only to the grand duke's antechamber and without seeing the grand duke

part was coined at the new mint and part at the old.[18] By September 1577 all silver pieces were coined at the new mint "by the hand of the Germans," and thenceforward the following division of labor prevailed: gold at the old mint and silver at the new mint.[19]

As we have seen, in the two decades 1570–79 and 1580–89, the coinages of silver coins at the Florence mint reached the level of 5.2 and 5.6 tons of pure silver a year. These were very high levels and certainly uncommon for Florence but must be evaluated by looking at what happened elsewhere. The arrivals of American silver in Seville in the same two decades amounted to 112 and 210 tons of pure silver a year.[20] Thus the silver minted in Florence represented about 5 percent and 3 percent, respectively, of the silver that arrived from the Americas. Data for the activity of the Milan mint are available only from the 1580s, and we know that in the decade 1581–90 coins were minted at an average of around 13 tons of pure

---

himself. Like a good Florentine, however, his greatest preoccupation was not to lose the 16 testoni handed over to the grand duke, and he therefore mentions witnesses to the consignment with great care.

18. In the years 1576 and 1577, when both the old mint and the new one operated by hydraulic power were producing silver coins, the maximum daily production at the old mint was 128 kilograms of coins of popolino silver, whereas the new mint could produce 222 kilograms (ASF, Zecca 155, 156). The auditors of the mint accounts for the period 1578–81 noted that the new technology had reduced some production costs: "In this new mint—they reported—which operates with a water mill, there are fewer expenses in minting but more wastage." The wastage was valued on average at 16 1/4 grains per pound (about 0.24 percent). Five years later, reporting on the period 1581–85, the auditors found that the situation had improved and that the wastage at the new mint was reduced to 13 3/5 grains per pound (around 0.2 percent) (ASF, Zecca, Sindaci 19, 21, ins. 27).

19. ASF, Zecca 154, 155.

20. Hamilton, *American Treasure*, p. 42.

silver a year, more than twice the volume of the Florentine output.[21] In the decade 1560–69, the London mint, which at that time coined practically for the whole of England, minted silver coins at an average of 26 tons of pure silver a year. This average is influenced, however, by the exceptionally high volume of mintings in the years 1560–62 on account of the general recoinage decided on by Elizabeth I and her advisers. In the next two decades, 1570–79 and 1580–89, the level of silver output in London was in the order of 10 and 13 tons of pure silver a year.[22] Although they were overshadowed somewhat in the general picture of international monetary flows, the levels of Florentine silver coinages look still considerable in absolute terms. Five tons of silver a year for twenty years are not to be treated lightly, and the first question in this context is, Where did this wave of silver come from? To answer this, the most reliable direction is obviously afforded by the entries regarding the inflow of metal to the mint.[23]

In the 1540s and 1550s, that is, before the beginning of the phase of great expansion of silver coinages, the silver that flowed into the mint to be transformed into Florentine coins was generally in the form of confiscated coins and of coins legally imported, mainly from Siena, Genoa, Rome, Naples, Venice, Lucca, Bologna, and "la Marca."[24] Subsequently, however, Spanish coins came gradually to assume a greater importance. In mint register 190, c. 220, under the date 23 August 1552, we read

21. Cipolla, *Mouvements monétaires*, pp. 77–82.

22. Challis, *Tudor Coinage*, app. II, p. 306.

23. Metal arrived at the mint in the form both of coins and bullion, but the geographical origin of the bullion is unknown, except in a very few cases.

24. ASF, Zecca 191, c. 86 (10 February 1559): "Gian Girolamo Companini, banker of Pisa, should receive 299 lire 3 soldi, namely, 267 lire 1 soldo and 4 denari for banned silver coins delivered to the

that 6 Florentine pounds 9 ounces 21 denari (around 2.3 kilograms) of Spanish reals were brought that day to the mint together with Venetian and Roman coins. At that time and for a few more years, the Spanish reals were in a minority compared with the other coins brought to the mint for recoinage. The 1560s brought a radical change in the situation.

In December 1560, Raffaele and Giovanni Spinola of Genoa brought around 126 1/2 Florentine pounds (about 43 kilograms) of Spanish reals to the Florentine mint.[25] In the semester March–August 1562, around 10,925 Florentine pounds (about 3.710 kilograms) of Spanish reals were brought to the mint; in the same period the Florentine mint coined silver pieces for a total of 17,535

---

mint, and 32 lire 1 soldo 8 denari for reals"; c. 95 (2 June 1559): "Giovan Girolamo Companini, banker in Pisa, must have 77 lire 5 soldi 4 denari for banned silver coins"; c. 95 (9 June 1559): "must have 56 fiorini 4 lire 11 soldi 8 denari for an amount of silver consisting in cut coins."

Examples of Sienese coins brought to the Florentine mint to be turned into Florentine coins in ASF, Zecca 191, cc. 145, 147, 156 (years 1560–61).

The following example, relating to coins from different areas, can be considered typical (ASF, Zecca 190, c. 20v, dated 7 June 1543: "Piero di Nerso must have: for 40 lb. 11 oz. 12 denari of Florentine coins at 67 lire 19 soldi 9 denari per pound; for 5 lb. 6 oz. 11 denari of Roman coins at 64 lire 4 soldi 6 denari per pound; for 3 lb. 10 oz. 6 denari of coins from Bologna at 58 lire 4 soldi 4 denari per pound; for 1 lb. 11 oz. 5 denari of coins from Lucca at 52 lire 11 soldi 8 denari per pound; for 8 oz. 22 denari of Venetian coins at 66 lire 14 soldi 8 denari per pound; for 10 oz. 13 denari of coins from Siena at 60 lire 4 soldi 7 denari per pound." The differences in the price per unit of weight (pound) among the various coins depended on the fineness of the coins themselves. The Florentine coins brought to the mint by Piero di Nerso to be recoined were probably deficient in weight because of wear.

25. Cipolla, *Argento spagnolo*, p. 476.

Florentine pounds (about 5.954 kilograms) of popolino silver.[26] In the semester September 1576–February 1577, out of 8,870 Florentine pounds (about 3.011 kilograms) of popolino silver brought to the mint in various forms, around 7,500 Florentine pounds (about 2.546 kilograms) were in the form of reals.[27] A petition dated 11 March 1567 pointed out that "for several years now, the Florentine mint has coined a large quantity of silver and almost all from Spanish reals."[28]

Thus the phase of great expansion in Florentine silver coinages that had begun toward the end of the 1550s coincided with the increasing inflow of Spanish silver coins to the Florence mint. This correspondence clearly indicates the close tie between the expansion in Florentine silver coinages and the process of diffusion of American silver throughout Europe. Two things must be specified at this point. First, it must be borne in mind that the reals did not represent the only form in which American silver came to the Florentine mint. Besides the reals, rods, ingots, and weights of silver were brought that might have originated in Spain or anywhere else. At the same time, as far as the reals are concerned, although there is no doubt about their original source, the coins in question might not have come directly from Spain but indirectly via Naples, Milan, and above all Genoa. When

26. ASF, Zecca 192. Spanish reals were brought to the mint by the bank of Federigo de' Ricci, 2,274 kilograms; the bank of Carnesecchi and Strozzi, 823 kilograms; the bank of Gio. Battista de' Servi, 206 kilograms; Niccolò and Francesco Capponi, 205 kilograms; others, 202 kilograms.

27. ASF, Zecca 137. In the same period, silver was coined in the mint in the amount of 6,709 pounds (around 2,278 kilograms). The difference between this amount and the 8,870 pounds of silver brought to the mint was passed on to the next financial semester.

28. ASF, Zecca 115, c. 338.

in February 1574 the Florentine mint credited "Antonio Salazar e Lesme da Stodiglia" with 1,610 Florentine pounds of reals, it is reasonable to suppose that the reals in question came directly from Spain.[29] When Raffaele and Giovan Battista Spinola of Genoa brought about 126.5 Florentine pounds of reals to the Florentine mint, it is reasonable to suppose that the Spanish coins in question had passed first through Genoa and had then been exported to Florence.[30] However, the majority of the reals were brought to the mint by merchants, bankers, and silk and wool manufacturers, and in these cases it remains unclear whether they came from Spain directly or from Genoa, Naples, Milan, or the fairs of Lyons, Besançon or Piacenza, which dominated in turn the international exchange markets of the time. This is no idle question. The reals, the coins from other countries, and the silver ingots were not gifts to the Florentines. The question of the origins of what flowed into the mint involves the question of the trade balance and the balance of payments between Tuscany and various countries—Spain, Genoa, and Naples, in particular.

Unfortunately we know absolutely nothing either about the trade balance or the balance of payments of Tuscany. We know that as far as trade relations with Spain are concerned, a certain type of cloth similar to serge that was produced in Florence had so invaded the market in Castile that the Cortes asked Philip II to protect local manufacturing by banning imports. Philip did in fact prohibit imports of this cloth with the decree of 21 January 1565, but he opened the Spanish border to Florentine cloth again in July 1566, though making it

29. ASF, Zecca 124, c. 2 (1 February 1574).
30. Cipolla, *Argento spagnolo*, p. 476.

subject to the high duty of 6 ducati per piece.[31] Between 1566 and 1569, 1,476 pieces of Florentine serge were allegedly imported into Castile.[32] Serge was a very highly prized woolen cloth. Most probably Florence also sent silk and brocade to Spain. Florence at the same time imported wool for its manufacturers on a large scale from Spain. These products were not the only goods traded between Florence and Spain but they probably made up the main part. What then was normally the balance between imports and exports? From the correspondence of the Spanish merchant Simon Ruíz, the historian Ruíz Martin has gathered the impression of an unfavorable trade balance for Florence, especially because of wool imports, in the second half of the sixteenth century.[33] This fact would have engendered a movement of precious metal from Florence to Spain and not vice versa, yet Ruíz Martin himself shows by documentary evidence that silver was exported from Spain to Tuscany and Italy in general.[34] It is obvious that we are dealing with inadequate and contradictory

31. Ruíz Martin, *Lettres marchandes*, pp. CVIII–CIX; Lapeyre, *Commercio exterior*, p. 52.

32. Lapeyre (*Commercio exterior*, p. 53) corrects Ruíz Martin's hypothesis (*Lettres marchandes*, p. CIX) that 2,500 pieces were imported into Spain in the same period. On the number of pieces of serge and other types of woolen cloth produced in Florence between 1616 and 1645, see Romano, *A Florence*, p. 511: similar data for the sixteenth century are unavailable. In a report to the grand duke of 1628, the *sopraintendente* of the *Arte della Lana* in Florence cites the "loss of the serge business with Spain" among the various causes of the crisis in Florentine wool manufacturing (Lombardi, "1629–1631," pp. 8–9, n. 17).

33. Ruíz Martin, *Lettres marchandes*, p. CXXXI.

34. Ibid., p. XLIX. For the 1590s, Ruíz Martin estimates annual exports of precious metal from Spain to Italy amounting to around 6 million ducats.

documentation. Things are further complicated by the importance of Genoa, about whose trade balance and balance of payments with Florence we know absolutely nothing. It must be added that the monetary market at a European level was well integrated and the flow of money from one part of Europe to another was determined not only by international trade but also by the relative movements of interest rates and the prices paid by the various mints for metals and coins. Thus, for example, at the end of the 1570s, Spanish reals were increasingly irregular and showed deterioration in fineness, so that the Florentine mint became more cautious and paid lower prices, favoring instead the coins from Genoa and Naples whose fineness was more reliable.[35] This fact immediately reduced the inflow of reals to the Florentine mint while it increased the inflow of coins from Genoa and Naples[36] without there being any structural changes, as far as we know, in the Tuscan import-export.

35. See the observations in ASF, Sindaci 19 (28 February 1587): "To reduce the silver contained in [Spanish reals] to our fineness it was usual to refine around 2/5 of those coined, but since the fineness has deteriorated considerably, it is now necessary to refine about half of them, and for the sum refined one must allow the usual wastage of half a denaro per pound."

Ricci (*Cronaca*, p. 257) wrote that during 1579 the mint, "to earn more, has lowered the price previously paid for the silver, namely, seven soldi piccioli per pound. Lately it has gone so far that the reals that on the market were paid at 72 lire, at the mint are paid at 68 lire 6 soldi." The accounts in ASF, Zecca 218, confirm that the reals estimated at a fineness of 11 ounces 2 denari, which before June 1578 the mint paid more often than not at 68 lire 10 soldi per pound, after June 1578 were mostly paid at 68 lire 6 soldi the pound. The reals of a fineness of 11 ounces 4 denari, however, kept the price of 69 lire per pound.

36. ASF, Zecca 139, 217, 218.

A key point, however, seems to be the following: as we have seen in the preceding chapter, gold currency became rarer on Florentine markets in the second half of the 1550s and was progressively so throughout the 1560s and 1570s, until it almost disappeared during the 1580s, when the Florentine monetary system emerged in practice as silver monometallism. If we consider the massive gold coinages between 1525 and 1550, the quantity of gold coins that went out of circulation must have reached considerable levels both in value and volume. Since it is difficult to imagine that such a mass of gold was being hoarded, we must deduce that a large part of the silver imports had been paid for by gold exports. This, as we have seen, was the opinion expressed by Benedetto Busini and Napoleone Cambi, who declared themselves convinced that the Florentine gold scudi were sent "particularly to Spain, where it seems that all the silver currency is extracted . . . and also to Genoa, where all or the greatest part of the silver that comes into Italy ends up."[37]

That gold migrated to Spain was a hypothesis, and that part of it moved from Florence to Genoa was another hypothesis. The fact is that no one knew or knows with precision where this gold really ended up.[38] As far as Florence is concerned, however, the fact that over 90 percent of the silver coined in the mint between 1576 and 1589 was in the form of silver scudi (that is, silver piastre with a nominal value of approximately one scudo, or 7 lire) can be taken as at least an indication that

37. See app. 4 and chap. 4.

38. According to Ruíz Martin (*Lettres marchandes*, p. XLIV), in Spain gold currency was extremely scarce in that period; Gascon makes a similar claim for France (see *Quelques aspects du rôle des Italiens*, pp. 49–50).

silver coinages of the period were to a large extent a substitute for the gold scudi that were disappearing from the market.

The implication of this somewhat tortuous but, I hope, convincing argument is that the tons of silver that poured into Florence between 1558 and 1589 did not represent a proportional net increase in liquidity. This conclusion should be kept in mind, together with what follows in the next chapter, if the crisis that hit the Florentine economy between 1575 and 1590 is to be understood.

CHAPTER SIX

The Banking Crisis

From the beginning of the thirteenth century, at least in the most developed cities in Italy, credit played an increasingly important role together with coins in making up the mass of means of payment. Limiting oneself to the study of mint records and the movement of coins consequently can be misleading, and Florence in the sixteenth century is a case in point.

As we have seen, the mint records show a spectacular expansion in the coinage of silver from 1558 onward. The same source also shows, however, that the increase in silver coinages was partially offset by the decline in gold coinages. Coinages represented only one of the parameters that determined the quantity of money in circulation. Another parameter is the export and the melting of coins. We do not have precise quantitative data for these latter phenomena, only clues. These clues, however, as shown in the preceding chapters, lead us to suppose that from the middle of the sixteenth century gold coins left Tuscany to such an extent that toward the end of the 1580s the Florentine monetary system seemed to have become basically a silver monometallic one.

The gold drain, in real terms, means that the exceptional levels of silver coinages between 1558 and 1589 do not represent a corresponding proportional increase in the quantity of money on the Tuscan market.[1] But there is more to it than that. The available quantity of means of payment was not represented only by coins in circulation. What would be referred to today as M1 or M2 included even then bank money, that is, what is known today as deposits. In the Florentine market in the second half of the sixteenth century this type of money represented a percentage of the total quantity of money we are unable to estimate, but various indicators lead us to believe that it was fairly large. From the middle of the 1570s exceptional events in the banking sector drastically reduced this kind of money, so that despite the tons of silver coins the mint poured onto the market, Florence was strangled for about twenty years by a great scarcity of liquidity or, as it was expressed at the time, by an exceptional *strettezza* (shortage).

Unfortunately, although we have macroeconomic data at our disposal for metal coins, such as minting records, there is an absolute dearth of quantitative macroeconomic data for the credit sector. The history of Tuscan banking in the sixteenth century has yet to be written. Moreover, even if one managed to trace and study the account books of the major Florentine banks, that is, those of the Ricci, of Zanobi Carnesecchi and Alessandro Strozzi, of Giovan Battista de' Servi, of Averado and Antonio Salviati, of Luigi and Alessandro Capponi, of Niccolò and Francesco Capponi, and others, after immense work that would mean research for decades by dozens

1. Not only gold coins but also silver coins could be exported according to changes in the trade balance and the balance of payments. See, for example, what a Capponi wrote to the Spanish merchant Simon Ruíz on 19 October 1581 (Ruíz Martin, *Lettres marchandes*, p. 130).

of researchers, the resulting data would still be grounded at the level of the individual firms, with little possibility of tracing macroeconomic data. Let us try, however, to put to good use what little information we have.

Giuliano de' Ricci wrote, in his *Cronaca*, that

> after the ruin and failure of the Antinori bank and the Fazii bank, the bank of Federigo di Ruberto de' Ricci, managed by his son-in-law Marcello di Giovanni Acciaiuoli, earned itself a good reputation both for its good management and the size of its operations: it had such a good name that both public and private money flowed into that bank and it was really everyone's cashier; it expanded and restricted the market at will, and one can venture to say that there were no other banks that moved cash around except the Ricci's. They kept this reputation and this position from 1552 until 1573.[2]

That "both public and private money" flowed into the Ricci bank, so that this bank became "really everyone's cashier" was not rhetorical hyperbole: it is confirmed by the mint records. In the semester March–August 1562, besides other foreign coins and gold and silver ingots, Spanish reals for the equivalent of about 3,710 kilograms (10,925 Florentine pounds) of popolino silver were brought to the mint to be recoined into Florentine coins. Of this amount 1,234 kilograms were brought to the mint by the three great merchant banks of Carnesecchi and Strozzi (823 kilograms), Gio. Battista de' Servi (206 kilograms), Nicolò and Francesco Capponi (205 kilograms), 202 kilograms from a certain number of small dealers and 2,274 kilograms from the Ricci bank, which alone, therefore, brought almost twice as much as the

2. Ricci, *Cronaca*, p. 255.

other three large banks together.[3] In the semester March–August 1565 the mint worked almost exclusively for the Ricci bank: silver coins were coined for an equivalent of about 976 thousand lire, and the Ricci bank brought silver to the mint to the value of around 912 thousand lire.[4] Between September 1565 and September 1566 the bank brought gold and silver to the mint for an amount of around 676 thousand lire.[5] Between October 1566 and August 1567 the Ricci brought precious metal to the mint worth around 709 thousand lire.[6] In the period between September 1570 and December 1572, almost 63 percent of all the silver brought to the mint was brought by the Ricci bank. The only other bank that stands out for the importance of its deliveries, the bank of Luigi and Alessandro Capponi, brought only 13 percent.[7]

The examples that have been mentioned are not extreme cases. Wherever and however the mint accounts are examined, the same conclusion emerges, that is, that the Florentine financial market was dominated by a narrow, oligopolistic group in which the Ricci bank took the lion's share. This bank managed to control such a large share of the market that, as the chronicler says, it was able to determine "at will" conditions of "shortage" or "largesse" on the market.[8]

The chronicler attributes the success of the Ricci bank and its influence to the entrepreneurial capacities of

3. See chap. 5, n. 26.
4. ASF, Zecca 211, 291, c. 1.
5. ASF, Zecca 291, c. 12.
6. ASF, Zecca 291, c. 34.
7. ASF, Zecca 117.
8. "When the market is said to contract or to grow, it means that there is very little money or a great deal for the merchants to exchange" (Davanzati, "Notizie de' cambi," p. 163).

Marcello di Giovanni Acciaiuoli, son-in-law of Federigo de' Ricci. We have no reason to doubt that Marcello was a successful manager. It is also true, however, that the fortunes of the bank had a political origin. Federigo de' Ricci had been one of the main supporters of Cosimo di Medici. What is more, when Cosimo found himself short of money while preparing and waging war against Siena, Federigo lent him a large sum of money without interest, perhaps the equivalent of a hundred thousand silver piastre. As a later document reveals, "not only did the grand duke pay him back but having put in his hands all the administration of his treasury was the cause of Federigo's making substantial profits, and his business came to be regarded as the most important on the Florentine market."[9] In other words, Cosimo gave administration of the funds of the grand ducal treasury to the Ricci bank out of gratitude to Federigo for his help in a moment of need.

The document in question exaggerates the measure of Cosimo's goodwill. The administration of the grand ducal receipts and expenditures was not transferred completely to the Ricci bank. However, the Depositeria registers confirm that in those years the grand ducal treasury relied on the Ricci bank to a large extent.[10] This reliance is confirmed further by Giuliano de' Ricci, who

9. Biblioteca Nazionale di Firenze, Ms. Palatino 1187, "Memorie istoriche diverse." The document talks about a hundred thousand piastre, but in 1555 the Florentine piastra had yet to be coined. It may be that the author of the document, who was writing at a later date, meant the equivalent in his time of a hundred thousand piastre.

10. The reform of March 1554 concentrated the treasury services in one office, known as the *Depositeria*, which "became the most centralized paying in-paying out agency of the Florentine state" (Teicher, "Politics and Finance," p. 345).

writes that "all the money both public and private flowed into that bank, which was in reality everyone's cashier."[11] This explains the enormous quantities of coins and metal the Ricci bank brought to the mint compared with that brought by the other banks. The Ricci bank moved around not only banking funds, which as was typical for the time came from mercantile activities as well as from banking, but also part of the funds of the treasury. From what happened later it must be presumed that the managers of the Ricci bank used the public funds as a monetary base for a policy of credit expansion. The preeminence of the Ricci bank in the Florentine market must have lured the other banks into emulating its policy of credit expansion. During the 1560s the Florentine economy went through a phase of great expansion, and in all likelihood the prosperity was fostered by the credit boom.[12] The trouble was that the limits of sound banking behavior were amply overstepped. Things came to a head with a severe generalized liquidity crisis of the entire banking system. That is to say, when the client of a bank asked for cash, it happened more and more frequently that the bank was unable to pay in cash but paid with a *polizza*, that is, a written payment order similar to what is known today as a check, drawn on another bank with which the first bank had an outstanding credit. This second bank did the same thing, and the poor depositors were driven from one bank to the next without managing to obtain the cash they needed, or if they managed to get it, had to pay a premium, or *agio*.

11. Ricci, *Cronaca*, p. 225.

12. Galluzzi, *Istoria del Granducato*, vol. 2, p. 220; Malanima, *Decadenza di un'economia*, p. 295. Wool production during the whole of the 1560s and until 1573 stood at the relatively high level of 30,000 pieces of cloth a year. See Romano, *A Florence*, p. 511, n. 1.

A grand ducal decree of January 1574 exposed the situation in no uncertain terms:

> Some public bankers use very sinister ways in negotiating their transactions: creditors who try to recoup all or part of their credits are sent from one banker to another, nor can the customer receive the requested payment except in the form of checks or written endorsements or in petty coins so that often to avoid delays they are forced to pay agio of money at a certain percentage even though this should not happen.[13]

The chronicler Bastiano Arditi was more concise but no less effective when he described the situation with this picturesque expression: "the banks . . . only paid in ink."[14]

The inconvenience became particularly acute on Saturdays when, as an eyewitness remarks, "the *maruffini* of the woolen and silk manufacturers could not get the money [from the banks] needed to pay their workers."[15] The crisis was not felt only on Saturdays, that is, on pay day. It happened continually that a company needed cash for some important deal and the banks were not able to satisfy the request. This frustration caused conflicts that could break out into disagreements "with dissatisfaction and verbal altercation." The difference that arose between the Ricci bank and the Carnesecchi and Strozzi bank in the persons of their respective directors Marcello Acciaiuoli and Napoleone Cambi had particularly

13. Cantini, *Legislazione toscana*, vol. 8, p. 88 (7 January 1574). As we shall see in n. 18, below, the text of this ordinance of January 1574 follows that of July 1568 almost to the letter. The "petty coins" referred to are fractional coins of lesser value than the giulio.

14. Arditi, *Diario*, p. 123.

15. Ibid. *Maruffino* was the manager or minister of a workshop of woolen or silk manufacture.

serious consequences. The Carnesecchi and Strozzi, "having a great deal of business in Lucca, often needed cash to send there." On a number of occasions they tried to take out cash in "large amounts" from the account they kept at the Ricci bank, but more than once the Ricci bank had not been able to "count" (that is, pay out cash). "And more than once—the chronicler writes—this gave rise to dissatisfaction and verbal altercations between Marcello Acciaiuoli [manager of the Ricci bank] and Napoleone Cambi, manager of the Carnesecchi and Strozzi bank."[16]

The chronicler Giuliano de' Ricci puts the beginning of the crisis between 1573, the year in which Federigo de' Ricci died and Napoleone Cambi was appointed director of the *Depositeria generale* (treasury) of the grand duke, and 1575, the year in which Marcello Acciaiuoli, son-in-law of Federigo and the manager of the bank, died.[17] There is no reason to doubt that the death of the two leading personalities of the Ricci bank and, for reasons which we will see later, the appointment of Napoleone Cambi as *depositario generale* helped to precipitate the crisis in the Ricci bank and the Florentine banking system of which the Ricci bank was the most important element. However, the issue of a proclamation on 17 July 1568, using terms identical to the later and already quoted proclamation of January 1574 (which attempted to prevent the increasingly frequent instances of banks' refusing to pay in cash or paying after subtracting an agio), suggests that things had already begun to go wrong some years before the 1570s.[18]

16. Ricci, *Cronaca*, p. 255.

17. Ibid.

18. Cantini, *Legislazione toscana*, vol. 7, pp. 26–27. The relevant parts of the ordinance are the following: "The sinister way of

The ordinance of 1568, which obliged bankers to pay in cash when asked to do so by their creditors, aimed at the effects of the crisis, ignored the causes, and was thus ineffectual. The situation gradually worsened and came to a head virulently during the 1570s.

We have already mentioned that in 1573 and 1575 Federigo de' Ricci and Marcello Acciaiuoli, who had been the heart and soul of the bank, died. The cup overflowed with the nomination of Napoleone Cambi as director of the treasury in 1573. Cambi had been head of the Carnesecchi and Strozzi bank in the years immediately preceding and in that guise had had, as we have seen, unpleasant clashes with Marcello Acciaiuoli, stemming from the fact that when Carnesecchi and Strozzi tried to withdraw cash from their deposits with the Ricci bank, they found themselves faced with refusal. When Cambi took up his post at the treasury he realized that what he had been compelled to put up with at Carnesecchi and Strozzi he now had to put up with at the treasury as well—that is, when the treasury needed cash, the Ricci were not able to satisfy their requests and paid "in

negotiating used by some banks of the city of Florence was considered: they hold other people's money and when a creditor wants all or part of his money back he is sent from one bank to the next and is not paid except with promissory notes, and this practice is to the detriment of everyone. It sometimes happens that creditors, because they are tired and need to speed things along as much as possible, pay a premium of a certain percentage even though they are not obliged to do so." These facts having been considered, it was ordered that "all those who keep or intend to keep other people's money in their banks must pay creditors in cash when the depositors so desire, without sending them from one bank to another. It is also forbidden for anyone of whatever state, level, or condition to sell silver coins of His Most Illustrious Highness or to take a premium on them in any way." See also ASF, Leggi e Bandi, app. 65.

ink" with *polizze di banco*. Cambi, who already bore a grudge on account of his altercations with Acciaiuoli, was in favor of a strong-arm policy, and in 1576 put a stop to the privileges of the Ricci bank: "After many difficulties, in 1576, the public camarlingos were ordered not to accept *polizze di banco* in payment any more or to take cash to the Ricci but to the Depositeria."[19]

The consequences of this decision were what could be expected, and the chronicler describes them thus: "Thence it has followed that from that time on the market has been left without money."[20] The causes of this phenomenon were seen by the chronicler to be in the government's budget surplus, which was no longer recycled by the Ricci bank: "Each month—he wrote—the surplus of the public revenues [is] being hoarded in the coffers."[21] The present state of research does not enable us to verify the chronicler's assertion: in other words, we do not know whether the government budget in effect closed with a healthy surplus and whether this was wholly or partially hoarded. It is not improbable.[22] What is certain is that a drastic credit squeeze did, in fact, take place. In all likelihood it was brought about by the Ricci bank. With the withdrawal of cash from the bank by the

19. Ricci, *Cronaca*, p. 256.

20. Ibid.

21. Ibid.

22. The Venetian ambassadors estimated that Francesco had a budget surplus amounting to the equivalent of around 500,000 scudi a year. Francesco put part of his liquid assets back in circulation, keeping "a good sum of money in the exchange market," equipping two galleons "that navigated for trade," and dealing in cereals. However, according to the Venetian ambassadors, a large part of his liquid assets were hoarded. Segarizzi, *Relazioni*, vol. 3, pt. 1, pp. 212–13, 261; pt. 2, pp. 20, 46–48. See also Galluzzi, *Istoria del Granducato*, vol. 2, pp. 460, 466, 469.

ducal treasury the bank was forced to restrict its credits;[23] the credit multiplier suddenly worked perversely, and the Florentine market was throttled by a liquidity crisis, induced by the credit squeeze, that was exceptionally serious both in intensity and length. In the chronicler's pages, in the merchants' letters, and in the contemporary bans we find continual, concerned references to the monetary and credit "stringency," to the banks that did not "count" (that is, did not pay out cash), and to the lack of cash to pay workers on Saturdays. Already in January 1574 a ban had been issued that echoed the previous one of 17 July 1568, ordering bankers to consider themselves "obliged to pay creditors in cash and good ducal currency without asking for any agio and without sending them from one bank to the next."[24]

The ban of course met the same fate as the previous one: it had no effect whatsoever. Early in October 1574 Bastiano Arditi wrote in his diary that "the banks' cashiers and other merchants and shopkeepers had difficulty in paying the poor artisans on Saturdays, because one could find only endorsed paper on the market." Things became so difficult in the two key sectors of the Florentine economy, wool and silk manufacturing, that

23. The chronicler Giuliano de' Ricci (*Cronaca*, p. 257) refers explicitly to a credit restriction of the Ricci bank but, unaware of the effects of the credit multiplier, he explains everything in terms of the substitution of one management group for another. In fact, the chronicler writes, the old directors of the bank, "being more aware than in the past, realized that the young directors had, to the disadvantage of the bank and their own advantage, been very loose with some clients and estimated them worthy of credits of more than 80,000 scudi. The heads of the bank all returned last December to pay closer attention to business than usual. They dismissed the young directors and followed a restrictive policy."

24. Cantini, *Legislazione toscana*, vol. 8, pp. 88–89.

Grand Duke Francesco was led to offer a loan of 100,000 ducats to "whomever did business."[25]

In September 1576, "in the city, there was great lamentation about the banks, which only paid with ink, and the workshops' masters were not able to get cash to pay their workers, who complained bitterly." Dissatisfaction was such that the grand duke, fearing a rebellion, fled to his villa at Poggio a Caiano "escorted by bands of trusted troops."[26]

In November of the same year the grand duke resorted once more to the discredited blunt tool of a decree that forbade the banks to "compel those who need to cash silver coins" to pay an agio to get the cash.[27] Some months later, in mid-February 1577, Arditi denounced "the disorder brought about by the dearth of cash, which was not available anywhere in the city, since banks did not pay those who had large credits with them and paid a pittance on Saturdays to the *maruffini*: so much that the poor workers went back to their families discontented and the city was filled with their complaints."[28]

By July "the shortage of cash" had become so severe that as an exception it was decided to allow the circulation in the grand duchy of Genoese coins in the form of silver scudi, mezzi scudi, and quarti scudi, thus making them legal tender.[29] Realistic as it was, and limited as it was, this measure represented a breach in Francesco's stern monetary program. The following year, 1578, as a result of "disorders and inconveniences" induced by "the banks' bad habit of paying by writing and not in cash," a further ordinance was issued that obliged bankers

25. Arditi, *Diario*, p. 26.
26. Ibid., p. 123.
27. Cantini, *Legislazione toscana*, vol. 8, p. 310.
28. Arditi, *Diario*, p. 143.
29. ASF, Leggi e Bandi, app. 65 (24 July 1577).

"to pay their debts in cash, not being of course forbidden to endorse bills whenever the parties agreed to it."[30] The same year Ricci noted that "every day one hears of new bankruptcies among merchants and new ruins among the tax farmers." Two years later, in 1580, he wrote that on the Florentine financial market "one does not find credit, there is no more cash, and nothing stirs anymore."[31] In 1581 a decision was taken to extend to the papal silver testone and to the papal giulio and mezzo giulio the permission to circulate in Tuscany that had already been granted to the silver Genoese scudi and their submultiples: all without any appreciable effects.[32] For most of the 1580s, the letters of the Spanish merchant Simon Ruíz repeatedly described the Florence money market as characterized, except for very short periods, by "great stringency and lack of credit [*grande estrecheza y falta de creditos*]."[33]

30. Arditi, *Diario*, p. 189n; Cantini, *Legislazione toscana*, vol. 9, pp. 130–33.
31. Ricci, *Cronaca*, pp. 249, 307.
32. ASF, Leggi e Bandi, app. 65 (11 August 1581).
33. Ruíz Martin, *Lettres marchandes*, esp. p. XCIII.

Epilogue

LIQUIDITY CRISES in the banking system, credit squeezes, growing scarcity of gold coins, which continually migrated from Tuscany where they were stubbornly undervalued, monetary revaluation in 1571 followed by an intransigent policy of maintenance of the new parity, and last but not least—if contemporary rumors were true—a policy of budgetary surplus with the consequent hoarding of masses of coins in the coffers of the ducal treasury: all these factors reinforced one another and beginning in the 1570s led in only one direction, to a drastic deflation. The price index calculated by Parenti is excessively weighted by agricultural prices, which were largely influenced by the vagaries of the climate; it is not therefore the best index with which to judge mercantile, manufacturing, and financial movements. It is however symptomatic that at the height of the so-called price revolution one finds a drop of almost 10 percent between 1575 and 1590 in the index.[1]

Other sources show that the housing market was also very badly hit. In 1582 the Venetian ambassador, Alvise Buonrizzo, reported that "real estate has fallen in price in the last few years more than 10 percent, because buyers are not to be found."[2] At a general economic level things were in such a sorry state that immediately after the death of the grand duke, the Venetian ambassador,

1. Parenti, *Prime ricerche*, p. 144.
2. Segarizzi, *Relazioni*, vol. 3, pt. 2, p. 20.

Contarini, wrote that Francesco had "reduced the city to great poverty."[3]

That in the last decades of the sixteenth century things did not go well in Florence is no novelty. At the end of the eighteenth century the historian Galluzzi wrote that "in 1580 a change began to be seen in Tuscany that was so unexpected that everyone was dismayed: trade decayed fast and bankruptcies were frequent."[4]

Galluzzi dated the beginning of the economic crisis at 1580 and related the crisis to the senseless grand ducal ordinance of 20 April 1582, which attempted to put a stop to the increasingly frequent series of failures by threatening whoever declared themselves bankrupt with imprisonment.[5] Recent studies have shown that already toward the second half of the 1570s there was a turnaround in the economic trend and the beginning of a long depression in wool and silk manufacturing and export.[6] Thus there seems to be a perfect chronological coincidence between the monetary crisis and the general economic crisis. By this I do not wish to imply that the economic crisis was determined by monetary policy. There were more general economic factors such as the backlash from the economic and financial crisis that between 1571 and 1590 hit the Lyons fairs in which Florentine companies played a very important role.[7]

3. Ibid., p. 42. Both Contarini and Buonrizzo (p. 20) describe the aspects of the crisis correctly, but they ascribe the causes simplistically to the budgetary stringency of Francesco, ignoring the effects of the monetary policy and the banking crisis.

4. Galluzzi, *Istoria del Granducato*, vol. 2, p. 460.

5. Ibid., p. 465.

6. Malanima, *I Riccardi*, pp. 56–57; and at greater length and more specifically, Malanima, *Decadenza di un'economia*, pp. 289–90.

7. Gascon, *Grand commerce*, vol. 2, pp. 572–82, 668–72, and *Quelques aspects*.

Moreover, long-term structural factors were gradually eroding the competitiveness of Florentine goods on both European and Levantine markets. However, the strict monetary policy that began in the mid-1560s and resulted in the revaluation of 1571 and the credit squeeze of the mid-1570s must have had a considerable impact. These monetary blows throttled the Florentine economy just when it was giving clear signs of extreme fragility and the need for a tonic.

A few months before his death in 1587, the grand duke Francesco assembled another commission to try to solve the by then ingrained monetary problems, which had afflicted Florence for years and which gave no sign of subsiding: the banks, especially the Ricci bank, continued to not "count" and depositors "could not get a penny of cash"; gold coins to pay bills of exchange were scarcer and scarcer and, if they could be found, had to be paid with a hefty agio in addition. This time the commission was formed by four experts, Bernardo Ricasoli, doctor in law, Napoleone Cambi, treasurer general, Vincenzo de' Ricci, one of the directors of the bank of the same name, and Jacopo Pintelli, the mint manager. The experts convened several times and discussed at length, but failed to come to a conclusion because they continually came up against the veto of the grand duke: "because the intention of the Granduke was firm in not wanting to alter the coinage either as regards weight or fineness. . . . Neither would he consent to the use of foreign coins."[8]

Thus Francesco remained faithful to his idea of monetary stringency until his death (19 October 1587), unshakable in his faith in the stability of monetary parameters, unaware of the crisis his attitude had helped

8. Ricci, *Cronaca*, p. 502.

to set in motion. On his death he left a paradoxical system: an economy in grave difficulties and a monetary system held up as a model by the other Italian states for its stability and correct alignment of metal parities, the draconian block of the output of fractional coins, and the exclusion, with few exceptions, of foreign coins from domestic circulation. Francesco's brother and successor, the grand duke Ferdinando, and his advisors had to solve the problems tied to this paradox. On the one hand, they realized that they must loosen the monetary noose that was strangling the economy; on the other, they were themselves prisoners of the tradition of monetary austerity that had become one of the myths of Florence and the Medici dynasty. They got out of it by compromising.

At the beginning of 1597 the parity fixed by the 1571 reform was inflexibly confirmed and Francesco's policy of the absolute stability of the metallic content of the Florentine coins was reiterated with no exceptions (see app. 3). Two years previously, however, in July 1595, the old mint of Pisa had been reactivated and allowance was made for the minting of coins at a slightly lower (around 3 percent) metal parity than the Florentine ones.[9] The

9. The text of the preface of 21 July 1595 reads: "Seeing that there has been scarcity of gold in Italy and elsewhere for some years now, which has caused and continues to cause the Florentine, Venetian, and Genoese mints to coin little gold . . . ; considering that the purity of the Florentine coins is such that whoever needs to extract silver currency for other states, mostly the East and some parts of Italy . . . does it at a loss. In order to increase trade and for the convenience of traders and other worthy causes, etc., it was ordered that the Florentine mint, according to its statutes and orders, should in no way alter the fineness or the value either of gold or of silver and that another public mint be erected in Pisa to coin the following gold and silver coins" (Carli, "De' vari generi di moneta coniata," in *Delle monete*, vol. 1, p. 347; Bandi di monete in the Library of the Fondazione Luigi Einaudi in Turin).

light coins minted in Pisa could be spent only outside Tuscany and were not allowed to circulate internally. As far as fractional coins are concerned, and the crazie in particular, the practice of strictly limiting the quantity in circulation was adhered to, but not in Francesco's draconian manner of stopping mintings completely and ordering the dies to be locked "in the safes and coffers." A certain elasticity was adopted by recognizing that a limited quantity could be minted for the "mere necessity of use and needs of the people" on written orders of the grand duke.[10] As far as foreign currency was concerned, on 11 April 1589, the spending of thirty-two carefully specified types of coin from the Papal States, Venice, Milan, Genoa, Ferrara, Urbino, and Lucca was permitted within the Tuscan state for a year.[11] On 3 March 1591 "considering how much benefit and convenience it has engendered . . . to grant that some foreign coins could be spent in the city of Florence and its dominions," it was decided to "enlarge that concession and allow many other coins to be spent in the said city and dominions"; the list of the permitted foreign coins was extended to sixty-two types of coins from the Papal States, Spain, Naples, Venice, Milan, Genoa, Ferrara, Mantua, Parma, Urbino, and Lucca.[12]

Thus only timid and extremely cautious attempts to loosen the monetary policy were made. At the same time it must be said that even audacious monetary maneuvers would not have sufficed to make up for the growing structural shortcomings of the Tuscan economy. Consequently, in the long run Florence continued its inexorable economic decline, while paradoxically its reputation for good monetary management remained intact.

10. See app. 3.

11. Cantini, *Legislazione toscana*, vol. 12, pp. 303–8.

12. ASF, Zecca 115, c. 417: "Provisione sopra la valuta delle monete et quattrini forestieri."

APPENDIX ONE

The Description of the Florentine Monetary System in Giuliano de' Ricci's *Cronaca*

At the end of the first chapter of this book only part of the paragraph of Giuliano de' Ricci's *Cronaca* that deals with the Florentine monetary system was included so as not to overload the reader with excessive technical detail. The paragraph in question, however, is worth quoting in full. Ricci writes (*Cronaca*, p. 67):

> Et perché gli si vegga come et di quante sorte monete et di che lega et a che peso si batte hoggi in Firenze ne fo nota qui appiè

	lire	soldi	denari
L'argento popolino sodo vale la libbra di 12 once	71	5	9
battuto se ne mette giulii 109 1/2 per libbra[1] et è a lega di once 11.12 per libbra.			

1. In the Sapori edition the pound sign has been mistaken for that of the ounce.

Vagliono detti giuli 109 1/2	73	—	—
Le monete sono le appresso et la lira è a soldi venti, il soldo denari dodici. Pesano tutte allo avvenante delle lire 73 per libbra: il piastrone o ducato d'argento che comunemente si chiama anco nelle scritture maxime fiorino, vale	7	—	—
il mezzo ducato d'argento	3	10	—
il riccio o vero testone	2	—	—
il cosimo o vero lira	1	—	—
il giulio, 2/3 di una lira et 3 giulii fanno il riccio	—	13	4
tutte le sopradette sono alla medesima lega di once 11.12			
la cratia vale cinque quattrini; è di peggior lega che sono che ne va 12 alla lira	—	1	8
il quattrino ne va 3 al soldo, vale	—	—	4
lo scudo d'oro in oro di grani 70 del conio ducale	7	12	—
lo scudo d'oro in oro d'altra stampe	7	10	—

The description of these coins does not raise any interpretative problems. It summarizes the monetary system as it has been described in chapter 1. The first few lines Ricci, who was by no means a paragon of clarity, felt it necessary to place before the list of metal coins, may need some clarification.

Ricci begins his description by stating that a Florentine pound of 12 ounces (that is, the pound weight of 339.5 grams) of popolino silver (silver of 958.33/1000 fineness) was worth 71 lire 5 soldi and 9 denari. This was the price the mint paid to whomever brought silver to be struck into Florentine coins, according to the reform of 1571. "From a pound [weight] 109 1/2 giulii are coined at a fineness of 11.12 ounces. These 109 1/2 giulii are worth lire 73." In other words: the mint paid whomever brought it silver 71 lire 5 soldi 9 denari a pound, but issued the equivalent of 109 1/2 giulii, that is, 73 lire. The difference between the 73 lire in coins that the mint extracted out of a pound of popolino silver and the 71 lire 5 soldi 9 denari that it paid to whomever had brought it the silver served to cover the minting expenses and yield a profit (signoraggio) that was then divided between the grand duke and the mint manager.

Having specified the facts above and before listing the metallic coins in circulation, Ricci noted that "the lira is at 20 soldi and the soldo 12 denari. All coins weigh 73 lire per pound." By this convoluted prose the chronicler means that henceforth he intends to express the nominal value of the various metallic coins in terms of lire of 20 soldi, each soldo being made up of 12 denari. As far as the weight of coins was concerned, he correctly states that at that time (that is, after the reform of 1571) Florentine silver coins were all put on the same footing, that is, that 73 lire weighed a pound in popolino silver whatever the type of coin. Thus, for example, the weight of the cosimo, which had a nominal value of one lira, was such as to make 73 pieces weigh one pound; the testone had a nominal value of 2 lire, thus 36 1/2 pieces were equal in value to 73 lire and weighed 1 pound, and so on. This applied to silver coins from the piastra to the giulio. Under the giulio, that is, with the mezzi giulii, crazie, black quattrini, and piccioli, this alignment was disregarded so as to be able to cope with the proportionally greater expenses of minting.

Ricci's text can be compared with that part of Giovan Battista della Torre's unpublished *Ragguaglio di Piazze* of 1600 that deals with Florentine coins (ASF, Depositeria 425):

> Firenze. Le sue piastre sono amate da per tutto né solo di par prezzo ma con differenza per la loro bontà per la quale hanno tanta fama fra le altre piastre quanto lo scudo di Spagna infra gli altri scudi.
>
> Ogni piastre 10 3/7 pesano una libbra di bontà realmente di oncie 11.12.

Questa piastra vale a piccioli	lire	7
mezza piastra		3. 10
il testone che è il doppio della lira		2
la lira che è il settimo della piastra		1
il giulio che è il terzo di questo testone		–, 13.4
gli mezzi giulii		–, 6.8

> Questi pezzi nella bontà a esse piastre sono eguali ma nel peso montano a punto quanto importa la fattura di fare di piccoli in piccol pezzo.
>
> Monete d'argento e rame questa piazza non ha che certe poche cratie perché non se ne batte del

continuo acciò che non alacrino bastando che solo servino nello spendere a minuto e nelle piccole divisioni.

Si batte per la medesima causa e del diminutivo quattrini di rame con un pocholino di argento che tre formano il soldo il quale misura tutte le soprascritte monete.

APPENDIX TWO

The Report of the Commission of 1571

Magnifici Signori di Zecca di questa Città di Fiorenza et tutti li altri Ufitali di quella, con la presente vi si notifica come havendo fatto relatione et quella tornata col rescritto in piede del tenore infrascritto, cioè:

Serenissimo Principe, Havendo Vostra Altezza commesso a noi sottoscritti che intendessimo et gli riferissimo il proceduto per l'adrieto da questa Ducal Zecca et ministri di quella et il modo migliore come per l'avvenire deve battere et coniare l'oro et l'argento, haviamo dato principio a trattare sopra di ciò et discusso maturamente quanto si è conosciuto che sia da fare per servitio di Vostra Altezza et de' suoi Populi et per augumento della detta zecca, havendo consideratione alle transgressioni preterite et per rimediare che l'oro sia conservato nel suo stato et che la moneta non sia peggiorata però che altro non fa salire in prezzo del oro se non il peggiorare della moneta oltre che quanto quella si peggiora tanto diminuiscono l'entrate di Vostra Altezza et per conseguentia li mobili d'ogni particulare; et per ubbidire a quanto Vostra Altezza comanda habbiamo concluso che

ASF, Zecca, Fiorinaio, cc. 190v–191r. Another copy in ASF, Zecca 115, c. 235.

sia bene per hora a tale che la zecca non restassi otiosa riferirli il modo come si deve fare osservare di battere et coniare l'oro et la moneta se a Vostra Altezza piacerà, cioè,

Havendo riguardo a l'uso et consuetudine de buoni ordini antichi et da quelli alienandoci il meno che sia possibile diciamo che

li scudi d'oro si debbino continuare di battere et coniare della solita lega di caratti ventidua col solito rimedio di mezzo ottavo di carato per oncia et ne vadia per ogni libbra scudi cento et mezzo coniati et finiti del tutto, et quando il ministro scoressi in fino in scudi 100 2/3 per libbra si comporti ma non piú oltre et che alla persona ch'avrà messo l'oro in zecca se li debbi rendere scudi 99 2/3 d'oro per ogni libbra d'oro di carati 22 et che lo scudo sia di peso di danari 2 grani 20 2/3 et ogni avanzo che restassi sia [della] zecca o ministri per supplire alle spese et altri carichi;

la moneta d'argento di qual si voglia sorte che Vostra Altezza destinerà battersi fondandosi sull'uso che per tanti anni s'è osservato di rendere a padroni dell'argento lire settantuna soldi cinque denari nove di moneta per ogni libra d'argento popolino, diciamo si debbi continuare di battere alla solita lega di oncie undici danari dodici per libra con un danaio d'argento per libra di remedio et ne vadia per libra giuli centonove e mezo per libra di moneta coniata e finita del tutto et non si comporti piú oltre e riuscendo piú di detti giuli 109 1/2 per libra li Signori di zecca non la possino né debbino licenziare ma subito farla disfare et rifarla di giusto peso. Et a chi haverà messo l'argento in zecca se li debbi rendere dette lire 71 [soldi] 5 [denari] 9 per libra et il giulio viene a essere di peso di danari dua grani quindici e uno ottavo e l'altre monete all'avvenante et ogni avanzo che restassi sia della zecca per supplire alle spese et altri carichi e cosí si debbe osservare inviolabilmente.

Considerato le transgressioni che in la detta zecca sono seguite nella tratta cioè nel liberare a patroni l'oro e l'argento coniato e per rimediare a disordini che nel peso sono per il passato seguiti, saremo di parere che li Signori di zecca o uno di essi almeno siano obligati intervenire e vedere pesare tanto li scudi d'oro che la moneta d'argento e non se ne stare né a parole né alla poliza del pesatore né aggiustatore ma vedere con l'occhio che non ne vadia per libra più di quello che di sopra è narrato. E similmente sia obligato il maestro di zecca con intervento de' Signori di zecca fare riconoscere, riscontrare et aggiustare tutti li pesi e bilance della zecca con li pesi e bilance del saggio ogni sei mesi all'entrare de nuovi Signori di zecca.

E tanto bisogna che Vostra Altezza li comandi di maniera che sia obedito et osservato e non incorrere per l'avvenire nelli medesimi disordini che per il passato s'è fatto e così restiamo baciando le mani di Vostra Altezza et in grazia di quella ci raccomandiamo.

Data in Firenze a di 30 giugno MDLXXI

Sta bene et cosí si metta in esecutione, 3 Julii 71.

E per tanto in virtú dell'autorità a noi concessa e visto il tenore del rescritto di Sua Altezza con la presente vi si ordina et comanda che da hoggi avanti debbiate in cotesta zecca continuare di battere e coniare li ori et argenti della lega e peso che in detta relatione si contiene e cosí dobbiate osservare senza nulla diminutione e non fate il contrario per quanto temete la indignatione di Sua Altezza et sotto le pene contenute ne vostri stabilimenti et altre pene reservate in mente di Sua Altezza.

Dato in Firenze a di 4 di luglio 1571

Marcello Acciajuoli,
Gio. Batista de Servi
Agnolo Biffoli
Giovanni Dini

APPENDIX THREE

The Report of the Commission of 1597

Serenissimo Gran Duca.

In esecutione di quanto ne impone l'Altezza Vostra Serenissima circa il ridurre in scritto li ordini della Sua Ducal Zecca di Firenze con li quali si habbino a regolare li maestri o ministri di essa senza alterare peso, lega o bontà intrinseca o estrinseca le diciamo che a un libro grande di carta pecora esistente in detta zecca dove solevano già notarsi le deliberationi che si facevano[1], si trova essere stato cominciato a copiare una relatione [del 1571] che si dice essere stata fatta da Marcello Accaiuoli, Giovan Battista de Servi, Agnolo Biffoli e Giovanni Dini sino in di 30 di giugno 1571 . . . e perché habbiamo considerato il tenore di essa [relazione del 1571] e le ordinationi che furono proposte da detti deputati con le quali la zecca dovessi seguitare di battere, e ritrahendo noi da Jacopo Pintelli, Pasquino Passerini, Lodovico Tempi saggiatore, il Buonaiuti pesatore e da Giaches Beliverth che si è andato osservando fino a hoggi quello che in esse

ASF, Zecca, Fiorinaio, cc. 191v–92.

1. The reference is to the mint book known as the Fiorinaio.

ordinationi si contiene e non trovando nella zecca scritture che mostrino deliberatione alcuna sopra che siano fondate le regole con le quali si è andata reggendo dall'anno 1571 in quà; e vedendo che in detto tempo si è pure battuto assai secondo la predetta relatione . . . accostandoci al tenore di essa et al seguito fin qui saremo di parere che in futuro si dovessi battere nell'infrascritto modo, espressamente prohibendo il contrario, cioè:

lo scudo d'oro sia alla solita lega di carati 22 col solito remedio di mezo ottavo di carato per oncia mandandone a taglio per ogni libra scudi cento e mezzo coniati e finiti del tutto e quando il ministro scorressi fino in scudi cento e dua per libra si comporti ma non piú oltre; et alla persona che haverà messo l'oro in zecca se li devi rendere scudi novanta nove e dua terzi d'oro per ogni libra di carati ventidua e lo scudo sia di peso di danari 2 grani 20 2/3 et ogni avanzo resti alla zecca e sua ministri per le spese e altri carichi;

e perché non troviamo che quelli deputati all'hora trattassino cosa alcuna del ducato gigliato e parendoci che anco di questa sorte di ducati si debba fare apparire nuova scrittura et ordine in questa zecca, le diciamo havere trovato che sino all'anno 1525 si sono battuti in detta zecca li ducati gigliati di carati ventiquattro e che ne sono iti a taglio ducati novanta sei per libra ma stante un rescritto fatto sotto dí 14 di maggio passato 1596 al supplicato di Riccardo Riccardi dove si trae che detti ducati gigliati si battino con le stampe solite da Lei già ordinate e della solita lega di carati venti quattro senza altro rimedio con mandarne a taglio ducati 97 1/3 per libra, non haviamo che dire sopra ciò.

La moneta d'argento di qualsivoglia sorte che Vostra Altezza Serenissima destinerà battersi fondandosi sull'uso che per tanti anni si è osservato di rendere a

padroni dell'argento lire 71 soldi 5 denari 9 di piccioli per ogni libra d'argento popolino, diciamo si debba continuare di battere alla solita lega di once 11 danari 12 d'argento per libra con un danaio d'argento per libra di remedio, mandandone a taglio per ciascuna libra coniata e finita del tutto giuli centonove e mezo né si comporti piú oltre et uscendo per ciascuna libra più quantità li Signori di Zecca non li possino né devino licenziare ma subito farle disfare e rifare di giusto peso—et a chi haverà messo l'argento in zecca se li debbi rendere lire 71 soldi 5 danari 9 per libra. Il peso delle monete deve essere cioè piastra deve essere di peso di once 1, danari 3 grani 14 4/5
meza piastra danari 13 grani 19 2/5
testone danari 7 grani 21 2/5
mezo testone cioè la lira danari 3 grani 22 7/10
giulio danari 2 grani 15 1/8
mezo giulio danari 1 grani 7 9/16
et ogni avanzo che restassi sia della zecca per supplire alle spese e altri carichi e che conforme a quello che da qualche dozina di anni in quà s'è osservato e che in detta relatione si tratta li Signori di zecca o uno d'essi almeno siano obligati intervenire e vedere pesare tanto li scudi e ducati d'oro quanto la moneta d'argento e d'ogni altra sorte e non se ne stare né a parole né alla polizza del pesatore o aggiustatore, ma vedere con l'occhio che non ne vadia per libra piú di quello di sopra è narrato . . . e similmente sia obbligato il maestro di zecca con intervento de Signori di essa fare riconoscere, riscontrare et aggiustare tutti li pesi et bilance della zecca con li pesi e bilance del saggio ogni sei mesi all'entrare de nuovi Signori.

Quanto poi al battere delle crazie troviamo che l'anno 1538 sotto dí 4 di novembre fu ordinato da Signori di zecca e nel 1542 confermato con autorità de Signori

Luogotenente e Consiglieri che dette crazie si dovessino battere a lega di once quattro d'ariento fine per libra con il remedio consueto e che ne andassino a taglio pezzi trecento diciotto per libra; sebene per il saggio che di esse ci riferiscono havere fatto di presente Pasquino Passerini e Lodovico Tempi s'intende essersene cavato di quelle gigliate, di quelle del San Giovanni giovane e di quelle della Lupa once 3 danari 20 d'argento per libra e di quelle del San Giovanni vecchio once 3 e danari 21 per libra e quanto al taglio secondo che appare a libri della zecca di quei tempi esistenti nelle mani de soprasindachi esserne state comportate da l'anno 1557 al 1560 inclusive da numero trecento ventotto insino a numero trecento trentacinque.

Quanto a quattrini neri haviamo trovato ne sopradetti tempi che li ordini detti erono a lega d'once una d'argento fine per libra ma che sono stati comportati a lega di danari 22 per ogni libra e ne sono iti a taglio per ogni libra da lire 7 e soldi 6 danari 8 sino in lire 7 soldi 11 danari 4 siccome appare a detti libri esistenti hoggi appo li soprasindachi. Et li diciamo che di dette crazie e quattrini non si doverebbe battere se non quanto ricerca la mera necessità e bisogno de popoli, ne senza espresso ordine in scritto di Vostra Altezza Serenissima perché sopra piú, stante la mala qualità di dette monete causeria disordine e danno allo avanzo dell'entrate di Vostra Altezza Serenissima e d'altri. Perciò sarà servita comandare quello che intorno a ciò le piace si faccia e noi humilmente baciandole la veste ce la raccomandiamo in grazia.

Della zecca il dì primo di marzo 1596 (s.f.; 1597)
Di Vostra Altezza Serenissima humilissimi servitori
Napoleone Cambi
Raffaello Vecchietti

Vincenzo Magalotti
Riccardo Riccardi

Sua Altezza approva tutto e conforme a questo e perché vi sia una regola certa con la quale li Uffiziali di zecca che per tempo saranno sappino qual modo e regola hanno a liberare l'oro e moneta che per tempo si batteranno, il Fiscale ne faccia distendere conforme al detto referto una provvisione del magistrato del Luogotenente e Consiglieri che lo vinca, la quale s'inserisca e registri ne libri publici della zecca dove chiami di nuovo quel Cancelliere perché tenghi conto di tutti li partiti de libri e ordini che si fanno per gli Signori di zecca e con miglior ordine e non con la negligenza che ha fatto per il passato. E quanto alle crazie e quattrini non si hanno a battere come ben dicono nel referto se non quanto importa la publica necessità e con rescritto di Sua Altezza la quale mossa da questo ha fatto battere queste poche ultimanente le quali costando che sieno di quella bontà che furono quelle ultime che fece battere l'Altezza Serenissima si possono liberare a zecchieri.

Il Gran Duca di Toscana, 8 di marzo 1596 (s.f.; 1597).

APPENDIX FOUR

The Report of the Commission of 1573 on the Exchange

Per ordine di Vostra Altezza Serenissima ci fu commesso che sopra il modo del cambiare noi facessimo chiamare alquanti mercanti pratichi con intendere quanto ne dicevano tanto in voce quanto per scrittura a fine che si provvedessi et ovviasse a' disordini che perciò ne potessino succedere, dove che per esecutione di quanto ce ne fu commesso habbiamo fatto ragunare nel Arte del Cambio la maggior parte de' mercanti che oggi negotiano in mercato nuovo et che trafficano giornalmente la cosa de' cambi; et havendo discorso et detto ciascuno la sua oppinione a parole si commesse loro che andassero pensando e che per un'altra tornata venissero in detta arte per discorrere di nuovo et per dovere lassare in scriptis quanto ne intendevano e che modo sarebbe loro parso di

A copy of this report may be found in ASF, Zecca 115, cc. 155–56. The 1573 report was included by Claudio Boissin in his report "Circa la valuta del fiorino," published by Argelati, *De monetis Italiae*, vol. 4 (with several mistakes in printing). Manuscript copies of Boissin's report are in ASF, Manoscritti 766, and ASF, Manelli, Galilei, Riccardi 434, ins. 11.

tenere in far detti cambi e che ciascuno di loro facesse il suo scritto; et essendo ritornati in detta Arte et poi che a lungho si fu discorso sopra detto negotio ciascuno di loro lasciò in scriptis il parer suo e come giudicavano che fusse bene governarsi in detti cambi, li quali pareri et scritti sono stati da noi letti et sommati e troviamo come appresso, cioè:

Alamanno de Pazzi — Guglielmo Nettoli
Carlo del Nero — Raffael Doni
Jacopo Martelli — Zanobi Carnesecchi
Marabotto Rustici — Ruberto Magalotti

Questi in sostanza dicono che si cambi et paghi a oro precisamente per dovere durare un anno o diciotto mesi et per cominciare a maggio prossimo.

Simone Corsi — Niccolo di Giunta
Galeotto Cei — Batista Cavalcanti
Filippo Antinori — Bernardo Pitti

Questi dicono che si cambi a oro overo in tanta moneta di argento dal giulio in su, pagando per ogni 100 scudi di cambi scudi 100 di lire 7 soldi 10 per scudo et pagando in scudi d'oro di buon peso li sia fatto buono a ragione di 3 1/2 per cento et che lo scudo d'oro si pregiasse lire 7 soldi 15 et che e banchi pagassino di contanti.

Marcello Acciaiuoli
dice che si possa pagare le lettere di cambio con scudi d'oro in oro di buona legha et peso a lire 7 soldi 14 l'uno et e ducali a lire 7 soldi 16 e quali cosí valutati sieno poi come la moneta grossa per servire alla valuta de'cambi, con un percento o quel piú o manco che fusse d'accordo con la parte.

Agnolo Guicciardini — Lorenzo Corsini

Raffael Niccolini	Tommaso de' Medici
Francesco Risaliti	Niccolo Mannelli

questi in sostanza dicono che lo scudo non s'accresca et che manco male sarebbe cambiare come si fa di presente.

Giovanni Manelli
dice che il cambio non si faccia a scudi d'oro, ma in nome di fiorini d'oro come e conti mercantili si tengono per divulgare il fiorino di lire 7 d'argento corrente di presente, et che li scudi ne' pagamenti de' suoi debiti ciascuno li potesse spendere e ne' pagamenti de' cambi per scudi 103 e soldi 12 e ne' pagamenti di moneta per fiorini 111.

Avendo noi deputati infrascritti

Carlo Pitti	Benedetto Busini
Napoleone Cambi	Giovan Battista de' Servi

visto quanto da detti mercanti è stato riferito, et havendo con lungha discussione considerato il tutto, siamo di parere che l'oppinione di quelli che vogliono alzare il prezo allo scudo o metterli aggio di 3 o 3 1/2 per cento non sia buona ma dannosa. Nel resto siamo d'oppinione come apresso, cioè:

Carlo Pitti e Giovan Battista de' Servi sono di parere e dicono che e' pagamenti da farsi delle lettere del cambio si mantengha il modo che di presente si usa et costuma e che chi non ha oro da pagarle li possa pagare in moneta ducale non minor che d'un giulio con uno scudo per cento d'aggio come per la legge del 1563 fu ordinato e per essersi in detto aggio di un per cento fattone mercantia si proibisca che non si possa pagare dette lettere di manco che detto scudo uno per cento et chi per qualsivoglia causa lo diminuisse o accrescessi di cosa alcuna incorra in pena di scudi cento d'oro o quella somma che paressi a Vostra Altezza Serenissima.

Benedetto Busini e Napoleone Cambi dicono et sono di parere che con difficoltà grandissima si potrà provedere che la piaza sia abondante di scudi d'oro perchè non è dubbio che chi ha li scudi fa eletione di mandarli dove vagliano piú et è chiara cosa che in ogni luogho vagliano molto piú delle lire 7 soldi 10 o lire 7 soldi 12 che sono valutati quí et particularmente in Spagna di dove pare che si cavino tutti li contanti lo scudo d'oro vale tanto argento che ridotto a peso et legha della zecca di Vostra Altezza Serenissima sono piú di lire 8 soldi 3 per scudo et conseguentemente a Genova dove capitano quasi tutti o la maggior parte de denari che vengono in Italia uno scudo d'oro vale lire 8 della Vostra moneta ducale o almeno tanto argento di lega simile a quella della Vostra zecca che vale lire 8 di questa moneta ducale o davantaggio.

Imperò per queste ragioni si conclude che non ci possa venire piú abbondantia di scudi d'oro di quel che per ordinario ha dato et da o darà le occasioni occorrenti se già non si alzassi il pregio dello scudo a pregio maggiore, la qual cosa ci pare pernitiosa perché si considera che la valuta cosí alta dello scudo in tutte le parti del mondo è causata dalla molta quantità di argento et poca quantità di scudi d'oro et se mai venisse, come pur potrebbe accadere, che venissi manco quantità d'argento et piú quantità d'oro, li prezi tornerebbono al lor giusto che è di lire 7 soldi 12 in circa per scudo.

Però non pare che sia bene incorrere in simile inconveniente d'alzarlo ma siamo d'openione che se non si può trovar modo da farci venire delli scudi d'oro, al manco si provegha il piú che si può alle difficultà de pagamenti cosí delli cambi come di tutte le altre cose; le quali difficultà, expressamente si conosce che nascono dalla bottegha che si fa delli aggi da scudi di cambi a moneta corrente e per tanto non ci piace l'oppinione di

Carlo et Giovan Batista perchè non vediamo che dia occasione di farci venire piú quantità di scudi e che nutrisce la bottega degli aggi dannosissima al universale. Et però siamo di oppinione che sarebbe manco male ridurre il modo del cambiare a ducati di moneta di lire 7 per ducato, che con questo modo ognuno saperrà come si potrà governare et fare il suo conto e sarà piú comodo a tenere le scritture et l'universale ne riceverà quiete et alcuni particulari non potranno agitare quelli che non sanno che cose sieno valute o aggi et detto modo di cambiare a moneta corrente sarebbe cosí admesso a Venetia, in Anversa, a Parigi, in Spagna, a Napoli, a Messina et Palermo. E se bene parrà che il levare al cambio questo nome di scudo d'oro possa parere innovatione di momento, non di meno se si considererà che questo nome di scudi di cambi, al modo d'oggi et che si è usato da dieci anni in quà et piú, è un nome che non ha sostanza vera ma sotto questa maschera si fa botttegha delli aggi et tutti li pagamenti si fanno a moneta, non pare che meriti molta consideratione né per quanto sarà che chi harà delli scudi d'oro o ne farà venire non possa farne i fatti sua come è seguito da dieci anni in qua. Et che per quella provisione del cambiare che fara Vostra Altezza Serenissima alterando l'uso presente, ci parrebbe che dovesse cominciare fra quatro mesi dal dí che sarà publicato quello sarà ordinato da Vostra Altezza Serenissima.

[Rescritto granducale] L'augumento dell'oro non piace in alcun modo a Sua Altezza né manco l'augumento del aggio di 3 et 3 1/2 per cento. Però proponghisi alli suddetti mercanti le due opinioni di Carlo Pitti e Giovan Batista de' Servi et di Benedetto Busini et di Napoleone Cambi e ben discusse tutte due riferischino quanto se ne ritrae da ciascuno. 7 gennaio 1573 [s.f.; 1574].

APPENDIX FIVE

The System of Weights of the Florentine Mint and Their Metric Equivalents

By a long-standing tradition, to weigh coins and metals, the Florentine mint used the units pound, ounce, denaro, and grains, which stood in relation to one another as follows:

1 pound = 12 ounces = 288 denari = 6,912 grains
1 ounce = 24 denari = 576 grains
1 denaro = 24 grains

When the metric decimal system was introduced into Tuscany the following equivalencies were established:

1 pound = 339.5420 grams
1 ounce = 28.295167 grams
1 denaro = 1.178965 grams
1 grain = 0.049123 grams

During the period dealt with in this book, both for technical and for more dishonest reasons (see chap. 3) measurements were not exact to the milligram or its fractions. Thus the calculations on which the discussion presented in this book is based have been rounded to the nearest tenth or, at the most, hundredth of a gram.

APPENDIX SIX

Half-Yearly Data on Gold and Silver Coinages, 1503–32

The two tables that follow, A1 and A2, illustrate how the data found in table 10, chapter 5, have been calculated starting from the data published by Bernocchi.

For the years 1524–25, the period covered by the data is the two and a half semesters from 1 June 1524 to 31 August 1525 (see table 10); thus the figure calculated as an annual average is less than the total for the period considered (15 months).

As far as gold coinages are concerned (table A1), when the amount of the minting is available it is specified that it was of florins, thus at a fineness of 24 carats. For the first semester of 1530, however, it is specified that "fuerunt coniati floreni et scuti aurei librarum 178 unciarum 5 denariorum 5" (Bernocchi, *Monete della Repubblica*, vol. 1, p. 471). The document does not tell us which fraction of the mass coined was in florins (of 24 carat fineness) and which fraction was in scudi (of 22.5 carat fineness). Since the sources are silent I have adopted the Solomonic solution of hypothesizing that half were florins and half scudi.

During the same first six months of 1530, 1,945 pounds of *mezi scudi d'argento dorato* (mezzi scudi of

TABLE A1. Gold coinages, 1503–32 (semiannual data).

Year	Semester	Coins minted (lb) (*a*)	Coins minted (kg) (*b*)	Fineness (carats) (*c*)	Kg pure gold minted (*d*)	Annual average (kg) (*e*)
1503	I	52.83	18	24	18	
	II	44.50	15	24	15	
1504	I	65.83	22	24	22	41
	II	40.83	14	24	14	
1505	I	96.42	33	24	33	
1510	II	76.58	26	24	26	
1511	I	72.90	25	24	25	62
	II	124.01	42	24	42	
1524 / 1525	II / I	950.66	323	24	323	258
1529	II	181.16	62	24	62	
1530	I	89.21	30	24	58	
		89.21	30	22.5		
	II	268.66	91	24	91	136
1531	I	78.50	27	24	27	
	II	449.58	153	24	153	
1532	I	47.25	16	24	16	

SOURCE: The data in column (*a*) are taken from Bernocchi, *Monete della Repubblica*, and are derived not from account books (which have been lost for that period) but from the mint book known as the Fiorinaio. For many of the missing semesters the annotations in the Fiorinaio indicate that coinings took place, but the amounts are not specified.

TABLE A2. Silver coinages, 1503–32 (semiannual data).

Year	Semester	Coins minted (lb) (*a*)	Coins minted (kg) (*b*)	Fineness (parts per thousand) (*c*)	Kg pure silver minted (*d*)	Annual average (kg) (*e*)
1503	I	1,099	373	958.3	357	
	II	1,994	677	958.3	649	
1504	I	1,439	489	958.3	469	958
	II	1,314.5	446	958.3	427	
1505	I	1,515	514	958.3	493	
1510	II	4,855	1,648	958.3	1,579	
1511	I	49.5	17	958.3	16	1,399
	II	1,548	526	958.3	504	
1524	II	783	266	958.3	255	204
1525	I					
1529	II	138	47	958.3	45	
1530	I	4,490	1,524	958.3	1,460	
	II	17.5	6	958.3	6	648
1531	I	136.5	46	958.3	44	
	II	166.5	57	958.3	55	
1532	I	1,024	348	958.3	333	

SOURCE: See table A1.

gilded silver) were also coined. Although these were intended to circulate as gold coins, I have included them in the silver coinages since the expression "gilded silver" leads one to infer that they were in fact silver coins.

In the mint accounts the first semester went from the first of March to the end of August and the second semester from the first of September to the end of February. The coining of gold scudi and mezzi scudi of gilded silver in 1530 must have taken place in the months of July and August, because the decision to mint these coins was taken in June of that year.

The coinages of 373.83 pounds of gold florins in the first six months of 1529 have been omitted from table A1 because data on the silver coinages for the same period are not available and their inclusion would have affected the average of column (*e*) and distorted the comparison between gold coinages and silver coinages.

In both table A1 and A2 the data of columns (*b*) are worked out by multiplying the data from column (*a*) by 339.5/1000. In table A1 the data of column (*d*) are worked out by multiplying the data from column (*b*) by those of column (*c*) and dividing the result by 24; in table A2 the data in column (*d*) are worked out by multiplying the data in column (*b*) by those in column (*c*) and dividing the result by 1000.

APPENDIX SEVEN

Half-Yearly Data on Gold, Silver, and Biglione Coinages, 1543–89

The data on coinages contained in the three tables A3, A4, and A5 are based principally on the mint series in ASF buste 116–120, 124, 150, 153–155, 157–167, 191–193, 197, 209, 213, 215, 217, 247, 248. Other data have been found in b 16, 19, and 21 of the Sindaci and Soprasindaci series. The data relate to the mintings of gold coins (table A3), of silver coins (table A4), and of petty coins or biglione (table A5). In all three tables the chronological ordering of the original sources on a half-yearly basis has been followed. According to the usage in the Florentine mint, the first semester of a given year went from 1 March to 31 August and the second semester went from the beginning of September to the end of February.

The layout of the three tables, A3, A4, and A5, is not identical because the data available for the various mintings are different.

Table A3 gives the number of pounds (weight) of 22 carat gold worked by the mint and the corresponding number of gold scudi minted. Figures do not indicate the actual number of pieces of 1 scudo minted. In addition to pieces of 1 scudo, pieces of a quarter of a scudo,

TABLE A3. Gold coinages, 1543–89 (semiannual data).

Year	Semester	Lbs. 22 carat gold	No. of gold scudi minted
1543	I	330	32,997
	II	197	19,697
1544	I	212.50	21,251
	II	139.25	13,925
1545	I	183.25	18,325
	II	337.50	33,775
1546	I	249	24,900
	II	187.75	18,771
1547	I	113.50	11,350
	II	127.50	12,750
1548	I	189.75	18,975
	II	101.25	10,175 1/2
1549	I	84.91	8,534
	II	84.75	8,517 1/3
1550	I	84.33	8,475 1/2
	II	47.50	4,773 2/3
1551	I	75.16	7,554 1/4
	II	130.75	13,140 1/6
1552	I	106.50	1,070 1/3
	II	112	11,255 2/3
1553	I	105.42	10,594 1/3
	II	11.16	1,122 1/4
1554	I	321.25	32,285 1/2
	II	60	6,038 1/3
1555	I	83.42	8,383 1/2
	II	89.25	8,969 1/2

TABLE A3. *(continued)*

Year	Semester	Lbs. 22 carat gold	No. of gold scudi minted
1556	I	69.33	6,968
	II	300.32	30,183 1/2
1557	I	137.17	13,785 1/2
	II	55	5,527 1/2
1558	I	72.42	[7,278]
	II	67.50	[6,783 2/3]
1559	I	72.42	[7,278]
	II	113.50	[11,406 2/3]
1560	I	48	[4,824]
	II	122.50	[12,311 1/4]
1561	I	174.25	[17,512]
	II	75.26	7,563 1/3
1562	I	121.33	12,191 1/2
	II	108.66	10,929
1563	I	178	17,913
	II	58.50	5,888
1564	I } II }	44	4,444
1565	I	—	—
	II	—	—
1566	I	51.66	5,195
	II	65.66	6,610
1567	I	—	—
	II	62.66	6,302

TABLE A3. *(continued)*

Year	Semester	Lbs. 22 carat gold	No. of gold scudi minted
1568	I	13	1,322
	II	17.66	1,774
1569	I	?	?
	II	22	2,224
1570	I	49	4,939
	II	31.50	3,165
1571	I	36	3,605
	II	81	8,167
1572	I	30.50	3,067
	II	?	?
1573	I	18	1,813 1/2
	II	?	?
1574	I	14.50	[1,457 1/4]
	II	36.90	[3,708 1/2]
1575	I	48	[4,824]
	II	43.50	[4,371 3/4]
1576	I	12.25	[1,231]
	II	11.10	[1,115 1/2]
1577	I	16	[1,608]
	II	50.50	[5,075 1/4]
1578	I	55.50	[5,577 3/4]
	II	37	3,718
1579	I	6.50	653 1/4
	II	31	3,115 1/2

TABLE A3. *(continued)*

Year	Semester	Lbs. 22 carat gold	No. of gold scudi minted
1580	I	41	4,120 1/2
	II	196.50	19,748 1/4
1581	I	45.50	4,572 3/4
	II	23.50	2,361 2/3
1582	I	23.50	2,361 2/3
	II	14	1,407
1583	I	—	—
	II	13	1,306 1/2
1584	I	6	603
	II	47	4,723 1/2
1585	I	9	904 1/2
	II	—	—
1586	I	—	—
	II	20.80	2,094
1587	I	11.20	1,130
	II	42.50	4,271 1/2
1588	I	3	302
	II	110	11,055
1589	I	—	—
	II	12	1,206

SOURCE: ASF, Zecca.

half a scudo, 2 scudi, and 10 scudi were coined. The figures provided in the table represent the total equivalent in scudi of the mass of the various gold denominations issued. In table A3, when the number of scudi coined appears in brackets it means that the figure is not given by the source but has been calculated on the basis of information relating to the pounds of metal coined. Since we do not know the market rate for the scudo except for very limited periods, although we know that the official rate was below the market rate, it is impossible to calculate a series that gives the value of the gold coinages in Florentine money of account (lire). However, if we consider that the scudo was also legal tender, one can argue that table A3 gives both the volume (pounds of gold of 22 carats) and value (in gold scudi) of the Florentine gold coinages in the period 1543–89. If we wish to make a comparison between the value of gold coinages and the value of silver and biglione ones we must translate the values of gold issues in scudi in values expressed in the Florentine money of account (lire). We have already said that series of rates of exchange of the scudo in Florentine lire are not available. In order to obtain rough orders of magnitude the reader can refer to the official exchange rate between the scudo and the lira of account as given in table 8.

Table A4 column (*a*) gives the volume of silver coinages expressed in pounds (weight) of silver at a constant fineness (958.3/1000). The documents usually give us the value in terms of Florentine lire of account of the money produced (col. [*b*]) from the mass of metal worked (col. [*a*]). By dividing the data from column (*b*) (value of output) by the data corresponding to column (*a*) (weight in pounds of silver worked) one obtains the average value, in lire, of the coins minted from a pound of popolino silver (col. [*c*]). The figures in column (*c*) are therefore an

TABLE A4. Silver coinages, 1543–89 (semiannual data).

Year	Semester	Lbs. popolino silver (958.3/1000) minted (*a*)	Value of coins minted (in thousands of lire) (*b*)	Lire produced per lb. of popolino silver (958.3/1000) (*c*) = (*b*)/(*a*)	Pure silver (1000/1000) parity of 1 lira in gm (*d*)
1543	I	4,321	304.9	70.6	4.6
	II	1,587	112	70.6	
1544	I	985	69.5	70.6	
	II	194.50	13.7	70.4	
1545	I	776.50	54.8	70.6	
	II	268	18.9	70.6	
1546	I	2,279	160.3	70.4	
	II	196	13.8	70.4	
1547	I	63	4.4	70.5	
	II	71	5.0	70.5	
1548	I	668	47.1	70.6	
	II	873.50	61.6	70.5	
1549	I	8	0.6	70.6	
	II	7	0.5	71.2	
1550	I	22.50	1.6	70.4	4.6
	II	21	1.5	71	
1551	I	6	0.4	71.2	
	II	764	54.9	71.8	
1552	I	934	67.1	71.9	
	II	886.50	63.6	71.7	

TABLE A4. *(continued)*

Year	Semester	Lbs. popolino silver (958.3/1000) minted (*a*)	Value of coins minted (in thousands of lire) (*b*)	Lire produced per lb. of popolino silver (958.3/1000) (*c*) = $\frac{(b)}{(a)}$	Pure silver (1000/1000) parity of 1 lira in gm (*d*)
1553	I	53.50	3.8	71.7	
	II	—	—	—	
1554	I	2,014	144.8	71.9	
	II	—	—	—	
1555	I	219	15.7	71.8	4.5
	II	167	12.0	71.7	
1556	I	?	?		
	II	?	?		
1557	I	?	?		
	II	90.50			
1558	I	2,970.50			
	II	8,067.50			
1559	I	2,169			
	II	3,264.50			
1560	I	66.50			
	II	1,037			
1561	I	417			
	II	1,897.50	138.1	72.8	
1562	I	17,534.50	1,274.6	72.7	
	II	295	21.4	72.7	

TABLE A4. *(continued)*

Year	Semester	Lbs. popolino silver (958.3/ 1000) minted (*a*)	Value of coins minted (in thousands of lire) (*b*)	Lire produced per lb. of popolino silver (958.3/ 1000) (*c*) = $\frac{(b)}{(a)}$	Pure silver (1000/1000) parity of 1 lira in gm (*d*)
1563	I	3,560.50	259.3	72.8	
	II	4,253	328.9	72.7	
1564	I II	9,076.50	660.1	72.7	
1565	I	13,287	975.8	73.4	4.4
	II	6,955.50	511.4	73.5	
1566	I	6,155	452.6	73.5	
	II	4,499.50	329.7	73.3	
1567	I	7,094	520.4	73.4	
	II	255	18.7	73.5	
1568	I	359.75	26.5	73.6	
	II	3,579	262.5	73.4	
1569	I	4,365.50	320.9	73.5	
	II	?	?		
1570	I	2,790	205.3	73.6	4.4
	II	7,395.50	543.8	73.5	
1571	I	13,647.25	997.3	73.1	
	II	5,337.50	385.7	72.3	4.5
1572	I	12,578.50	916.2	72.8	
	II	14,937	1,088.6	72.9	

TABLE A4. *(continued)*

Year	Semester	Lbs. popolino silver (958.3/1000) minted (*a*)	Value of coins minted (in thousands of lire) (*b*)	Lire produced per lb. of popolino silver (958.3/1000) (*c*) = (*b*)/(*a*)	Pure silver (1000/1000) parity of 1 lira in gm (*d*)
1573	I	10,209.50	745.3	73.0	
	II	16,259	1,185.8	72.9	
1574	I	7,725.50	563.5	72.9	
	II	1,060.17	77.3	72.9	
1575	I	5,185.50	378.0	72.9	4.5
	II	169	12.3	73.0	
1576	I	762.50	55.7	73.1	
	II	6,709	490.1	73.1	
1577	I	9,871.50	724.1	73.4	
	II	10,674	779.5	73.0	
1578	I	10,169.50	742.7	73.0	
	II	3,866.50	284.6	73.6	
1579	I	17,743.50	1,296.6	73.1	
	II	1,231	90.3	73.4	
1580	I	668	48.8	73.1	4.5
	II	337.50	24.8	73.5	
1581	I	46	3.4	73.0	
	II	2,768.50	202.3	73.1	
1582	I	6,175	451	73.0	
	II	2,335	170.5	73.0	

TABLE A4. *(continued)*

Year	Semester	Lbs. popolino silver (958.3/1000) minted (*a*)	Value of coins minted (in thousands of lire) (*b*)	Lire produced per lb. of popolino silver (958.3/1000) (*c*) = (*b*)/(*a*)	Pure silver (1000/1000) parity of 1 lira in gm (*d*)
1583	I	4,707.50	343.9	73.0	
	II	5,300	387.1	73.1	
1584	I	13,657.50	997.7	73.1	
	II	15,350.50	1,121	73.0	
1585	I	12,895.50	941.7	73.0	4.5
	II	8,605	628.4	73.0	
1586	I	19,483.50	1,422.8	73.0	
	II	7,787.50	568.7	73.0	
1587	I	11,849	865.3	73.0	
	II	6,048	441.7	73.0	
1588	I	22,162.50	1,618.6	73.0	
	II	9,315	680.3	73.0	
1589	I	10,202.50	745.1	73.0	
	II	11,946.50	872.5	73.0	

index of the stability or the instability of the silver coinage. On the basis of the data in column (*c*) I have calculated the metallic parity of the Florentine lira expressed in grams of pure silver (1000/1000) for the beginning of every decade and for 1571, the year of the report of the four experts (col. [*d*]).

Table A5 gives the value expressed in Florentine lire of account of the output of coins of low fineness, such as crazie, white quattrini, black quattrini, and denari, known as piccioli. The numbers in brackets have been calculated on the basis of the amount of metal worked.

In tables A3, A4, and A5 the question marks indicate that for the corresponding year we do not know if coinages took place or if the information we have is complete. The dashes indicate that there were no coinages.

TABLE A5. Value of biglione coinages, 1543–89 (semiannual data).

Year	Semester	Crazie (thousands of lire)	Quattrini and piccioli (thousands of lire)	Total
1543	I	68	5	73
	II	31	4	35
1544	I	53	5	58
	II	41	15	56
1545	I	3	9	12
	II	35	8	43
1546	I	56	—	56
	II	5	2	7
1547	I	—	4	4
	II	3	1	4
1548	I	1	1	2
	II	7	2	9
1549	I	2	3	5
	II	2	1	3

TABLE A5. *(continued)*

Year	Semester	Crazie (thousands of lire)	Quattrini and piccioli (thousands of lire)	Total
1550	I	4	4	8
	II	2	2	4
1551	I	4	2	6
	II	1	2	3
1552	I	1	4	5
	II	1	3	4
1553	I	4	1	5
	II	4	1	5
1554	I	2	—	2
	II	7	—	7
1555	I	3	1	4
	II	28	1	29
1556	I	3	2	5
	II	1	?	?
1557	I	1	?	?
	II	4	?	?
1558	I	5	?	?
	II	?	?	?
1559	I	9	?	?
	II	22	?	?
1560	I	28	?	?
	II	109	?	?
1561	I	141	?	?
	II	6	6	12

TABLE A5. *(continued)*

Year	Semester	Crazie (thousands of lire)	Quattrini and piccioli (thousands of lire)	Total
1562	I	1	—	1
	II	?	1	?
1563	I	4	—	4
	II	—	—	—
1564–88		—	—	—
1589	I	—	3	3
	II	—	1	1

APPENDIX EIGHT

Calculation of the Annual Average Volume of Gold and Silver Coinages for Selected Periods, 1543–89

The two tables which follow, A6 and A7, illustrate the steps taken to calculate the data in table 11, chapter 5, starting from the half-yearly data of the tables in appendix 7.

In table A6 the data in column (*a*) are derived from the data in column 3 of table A3, in appendix 7. The data in column (*b*) have been calculated dividing the data in column (*a*) by the number of years included in the corresponding period. The data of the following column have been calculated as follows:

$$(c) = (b) \times 339.5/1000$$
$$(d) = (c) \times 22/24$$

As to table A7, the data in column (*a*) are based on the data in column (*a*) of table A4 of appendix 7. The data in column (*b*) have been calculated by dividing the data in column (*a*) by the number of years included in the corresponding period. The data of the following columns have been calculated as follows:

$$(c) = (b) \times 339.5/1000$$
$$(d) = (c) \times 958.3/1000$$

The parameter 339.5 represents the number of grams equivalent to the Florentine pound weight. The parameter 22/24 represents the fineness of the gold scudi. The parameter 958.3/1000 represents the fineness of popolino silver.

TABLE A6. Volume of gold coinages, 1543–89.

Period	Lbs. of gold alloy minted (*a*)	Lbs. of gold alloy minted (annual averages) (*b*)	Kg of fineness of gold alloy minted (annual averages) (*c*)	Kg of pure gold minted (annual averages) (*d*)
1543–49	2,538	363	123	113
1550–57	1,789	224	76	70
1558–59	326	163	55	50
1560–69	1,163	122	41	36
1570–79	609*	68*	23	21
1580–89	618	62	21	19

*Data for two semesters are missing.

TABLE A7. Volume of silver coinages, 1543–89.

Period	Lbs. of popolino silver minted (*a*)	Lbs. of popolino silver minted (annual averages) (*b*)	Kg of popolino silver minted (annual averages) (*c*)	Kg of pure silver minted (annual averages) (*d*)
1543–49	12,298	1,757	597	572
1550–57*	5,178	797*	271	260
1558–59	16,472	8,236	2,796	2,679
1560–69**	84,714	8,914**	3,028	2,902
1570–79	158,346	15,835	5,376	5,152
1580–89	171,641	17,164	5,827	5,584

* Data for the three semesters from 1 March 1556 to 31 August 1557 are missing.

** Data for the semester from 1 September 1569 to 28 February 1570 are missing.

Bibliography

Angiolini, F. "L'arsenale mediceo: La politica marittima dei Medici e le vicende dell'arsenale a Pisa." In *Livorno e Pisa: Due città e un territorio nella politica dei Medici*. Pisa, 1980.

Arditi, B. *Diario di Firenze e di altri parti della Cristianità (1574–1579)*. Ed. R. Cantagalli. Florence, 1970.

Argelati, F., ed. *De monetis Italiae variorum illustrium virorum dissertationes*. Milan, 1750–59.

Bernocchi, M. *Le monete della Repubblica fiorentina*. 4 vols. Florence, 1974–78.

Blanchet, A., and A. Dieudonné. *Manuel de numismatique française*. 2 vols. Paris, 1912–16.

Boissin, C. "Risposta di messer Claudio Boissin circa la valuta del fiorino." In *De monetis Italiae*, ed. Argelati, vol. 4.

Braudel, F. *La Méditerranée et le monde méditerranéen à l'époque de Philippe II*. Paris, 1949.

Cantini, L. *Legislazione toscana raccolta e illustrata*. Florence, 1800–1807.

Carli, G. R. *Delle monete e dell'instituzione delle zecche d'Italia*. Vol. 1, Mantua, 1754. Vol. 2, Pisa, 1757. Vol. 3, Lucca, 1760.

Challis, C. E. "Spanish Bullion and Monetary Inflation in England in the Later Sixteenth Century." *Journal of European Economic History* 4 (1975): 381–92.

———. *The Tudor Coinage*. Manchester, 1978.

Cipolla, C. M. *Mouvements monétaires dans l'État de Milan (1580–1700)*. Paris, 1952.

———. *Moneta e civiltà mediterranea*. Venice, 1957.

———. *Le avventure della lira*. Milan, 1958.

———. *Il fiorino e il quattrino: La politica monetaria a Firenze nel 1300*. Bologna, 1982. Trans. as *The Monetary Policy of Fourteenth-Century Florence*. Berkeley and Los Angeles, 1982.

———. "Argento spagnolo e monetazione fiorentina nel Cinquecento." In *Aspetti della vita economica medievale*. Florence, 1985.

———. *La moneta a Milano nel Quattrocento*. Rome, 1988.

Cochrane, E. *Florence in the Forgotten Centuries, 1527–1800*. Chicago, 1973.

Corpus Nummorum Italicorum. 20 vols. Rome, 1910–43.

Dasí, T. *Estudio de los reales de a ocho*. Valencia, 1850.

Davanzati, B. "Notizie de' cambi." In *Scisma d'Inghilterra con altre operette*. Milan, 1807.

Diaz, F. *Il Granducato di Toscana*. Turin, 1976.

Galeotti, A. *Le monete del Granducato di Toscana*. Leghorn, 1930.

Galluzzi, R. *Istoria del Granducato di Toscana sotto il governo della casa Medici*. 5 vols. Florence, 1781.

Gascon, R. "Quelques aspects du rôle des Italiens dans la crise des foires de Lyon du dernier tiers du XVI siècle." *Cahiers d'histoire* 5 (1960).

———. *Grand commerce et vie urbaine au XVI siècle: Lyon et ses marchands*. 2 vols. Paris, 1971.

Gaye, G. *Carteggio inedito di artisti dei secoli XIV, XV, XVI*. Florence, 1840.

Gianelli, G. "Problemi monetari genovesi del Seicento: La questione della 'moneta specifica.' " In *Scritti in onore del prof. P. E. Taviani*. Annali della Facoltà de Scienze Politiche dell'Università di Genova 11–13 (1983–86).

Gnecchi, F., and E. Gnecchi. *Le monete di Milano*. Milan, 1884.

Grierson, P. "Ercole d'Este and Leonardo da Vinci's Equestrian Statue of Francesco Sforza." In *Later Medieval Numismatics*. London, 1979.

Hamilton, E. J. *American Treasure and the Price Revolution in Spain, 1501–1650*. Cambridge, Mass., 1934.

Heiss, A. *Descripción general de las monedas hispano-cristiana*. Madrid, 1865.

Herrera, A. *El Duro: Estudio de los reales de a ocho españoles*. Madrid, 1914.

Jara, A. *Tres ensayos sobre economía minera hispanoamericana*. Santiago de Chile, 1966.

Lane, F., and R. C. Mueller. *Money and Banking in Medieval and Renaissance Venice*. Baltimore, 1985.

Lapeyre, H. *El comercio exterior de Castilla a traves de las aduanas de Felipe II*. Valladolid, 1981.

Lombardi, D. "1629–1631: Crisi e peste a Firenze." *Archivio storico italiano* 137 (1979): 3–50.

Malanima, P. *I Riccardi di Firenze*. Florence, 1977.

———. *La decadenza di un'economia cittadina: L'industria di Firenze nei secoli XVI–XVII*. Bologna, 1982.

Mateu y Llopis, F. *La moneda española*. Barcelona, 1946.

Meroni, U. *I "Libri delle uscite delle monete" della zecca di Genova dal 1589 al 1640*. Mantua, 1957.

Montanari, G. "La zecca in consulta di stato (1683)." In *Economisti del Cinque e Seicento*, ed. A. Graziani. Bari, 1913.

Orsini, I. *Storia delle monete de' Granduchi di Toscana*. Florence, 1756.

Paolozzi-Strozzi, B. *Le monete fiorentine dalla Repubblica ai Medici*. Florence, 1984.

Papadopoli, N. *Le monete di Venezia*. 3 vols. Venice, 1893–1919.

Parenti, G. *Prime ricerche sulla rivoluzione dei prezzi in Firenze*. Florence, 1939.

Peri, G. D. *Il negotiante*. Genoa, 1638.

Pesce, G., and G. Felloni. *Le monete genovesi*. Genoa, 1975.

Ricci, G. de'. *Cronaca (1532–1606)*. Ed. G. Sapori. Milan & Naples, 1972.

Richards, J. F., ed. *Precious Metals in the Late Medieval and Early Modern Worlds*. Durham, 1983.

Romano, R. "A Florence au XVII siècle." *Annales E.S.C.* 7 (1952): 508–12.

Ruíz Martin, F. *Lettres marchandes échangées entre Florence et Medina del Campo*. Paris, 1965.

Segarizzi, A. *Relazioni degli Ambasciatori Veneti al Senato*. Bari, 1916.

Segni, B. *Istorie fiorentine*. Ed. G. Gargani. Florence, 1857.

Spooner, F. C. *L'économie mondiale et les frappes monétaires en France (1493–1680)*. Paris, 1956.

Targioni-Tozzetti, G. "Del fiorino di sigillo." In *Nuova raccolta delle monete e zecche d'Italia*, ed. G. A. Zanetti. Vol. 1. Bologna, 1775.

Teicher, A. "Politics and Finance in the Age of Cosimo I." In *Firenze e la Toscana dei Medici nell' Europa del Cinquecento*, vol. 1. Florence, 1983.

Tondo, L. "La moneta nella storia d'Europa del '500: Il pensiero del Principe." In *Pistoia: Una città nello stato mediceo*. Pistoia, 1980.

Tucci, U. "Le emissioni monetarie di Venezia e i movimenti internazionali dell'oro." In *Mercanti, navi, monete nel Cinquecento veneziano*, ed. U. Tucci. Bologna, 1981.

———. "La meccanizzazione della coniatura delle monete e la zecca veneziana." In *Mercanti, navi, monete nel Cinquecento veneziano*, ed. U. Tucci. Bologna, 1981.

Varchi, B. *Storia fiorentina*. Cologne, 1721.

Vettori, F. *Il fiorino d'oro antico illustrato*. Florence, 1738.

Index

Compositor: Campaigne & Somit Typography

Text: 10/12 Palatino
Display: Palatino

Lightning Source UK Ltd.
Milton Keynes UK
UKHW020832051221
395058UK00008B/629